Easy to read and relate to, like ch
Claudia touches on tough care
will take you to the next level. As an entrepreneur with decades of experience, I'm always interested in practical resources to boost my business and elevate my mindset. Claudia's book *Take Charge* is a great asset to every executive and entrepreneur's bookshelf! This book offers powerful business strategies, mindset shifts, and personal anecdotes that left me feeling inspired and equipped to elevate my business.

— **Diana Richardson**, Business Strategist, Catalyst Coach & Visionary, Signature D Ltd & Glowgetter Beauty Entrepreneurs

Claudia Thompson's *Take Charge* is a game-changer for small business owners seeking to inspire and empower their teams. I particularly love her practical BOSS method that offers business leaders actionable strategies to create a workplace where people actually WANT to be!

Thompson's clear guidance addresses real challenges in a welcome, empathic style to help build a team culture rooted in trust.

I believe that this book doesn't just teach Leadership, it reignites passion for business, making it an essential read for anyone eager to lead with confidence, clarity — and create extraordinary results.

— **Andy Edwards**, International Speaker and Author of *LEADERSHIT*

Claudia offers excellent wisdom and practical knowledge for leaders who want to transform their teams. Her thoughts on engagement, culture and team dynamics are invaluable for anyone looking to unlock the full potential of their people and create workplaces that inspire.

— **Jamil Qureshi**, International Speaker and Author of *The Mind Couch* and *The Secret Footballer How To Win. Lessons from the Premier League*

So many entrepreneurs have great ideas, which lead to successful businesses, which then grow exponentially and before they know it, they are managers of people, whether they wanted to be or not.

Claudia Thompson's *Take Charge* equips business owners with the tools and insight they need to become great people leaders. Not just a book on theory, *Take Charge* offers a well thought out, practical approach, with exercises and techniques designed to deliver real results.

The added bonus is Claudia's personal, pragmatic and often humorous style, which ensures an engaging read.

— **Andrew Halford**, Director Consultant, Pink Fluff HR Consultancy

The advice and guidance in *Take Charge* has been vital in my journey from a solo entrepreneur to building and growing my team. This book provides all hints, tips, clear step-by-step guidance and frameworks for me to follow having never led a team before. I recommend to any small business owners/leaders to read, that currently has or is thinking about a team.

— **Jennifer Horler**, Founder, Lionheart Virtual Assistance

Claudia's book is refreshing. It's a straightforward accessible guide to aid team engagement and team development, written in a clear, easy-to-follow style. Take Charge delivers valuable insights without unnecessary complexity, making it a great resource to support all levels of leader.

At the heart of *Take Charge* is the 'BOSS' method, which provides a practical approach to strengthen teams and build workplace dynamics. The integral exercises are well thought out, to encourage natural reflection and all-important action.

— **Carly Warren**, Managing Director, Thoroughbred Marketing

TAKE CHARGE

The BOSS method© for entrepreneurs
who never planned to be leaders

CLAUDIA D. THOMPSON

Copyright © Claudia D. Thompson 2025. All rights reserved.

This book or any portion thereof may not be reproduced or used in any manner whatsoever without the express written permission of the publisher except for the use of brief quotations in a book review.

Strenuous attempts have been made to credit all copyrighted materials used in this book. All such materials and trademarks, which are referenced in this book, are the full property of their respective copyright owners. Every effort has been made to obtain copyright permission for material quoted in this book. Any omissions will be rectified in future editions.

Cover image by: Nenad Cvetkovski
Book design by: SWATT Books Ltd

Printed in the United Kingdom
First Printing, 2025

ISBN: 978-1-0684461-0-8 (Paperback)
ISBN: 978-1-0684461-1-5 (eBook)

Cloud & Claw
South Petherton, Somerset

www.takecharge-thebook.com

Contents

Foreword 7

Introduction 11

1. **Be the Boss Your Business Needs** 21
   Am I a leader? Am I a manager? 24
   Where has my mojo gone? 37
   Build-a-boss 46
   It's not just about sweet talking 49
   Stop doing this:
   Ditch these habits for a happier team 53

2. **Organise the Ideal** 65
   Where are you going? 66
   What are you doing? 74
   How are you doing it? 83
   How to make it stick 94

3. **Survey the Current Reality** 103
   Who are you working with? 104
   What are they doing? 121
   The organisational structure 128
   Getting their perspective 131

4. **Strategise and Make It Happen** 147
　Getting everyone in position 148
　Making the rules for the team 153
　Making the rules for the individual 172
　Maintaining momentum 179

5. **A Final Word: You Are Exactly What Your Business Needs** 191

Acknowledgements 197

Further Reading 201

Endnotes 203

Foreword

Leadership. Well now, that's a word that gets thrown around a lot. It would seem everyone's got an opinion on what it should look like, how to master it, and the magic formula for getting it right.

Working with some of the biggest brands in the world has taught me that leadership isn't about company size — it's about clarity, confidence, connection and compassion. Claudia's book bridges that gap beautifully for small business owners, giving them the tools they need to lead with impact and purpose.

But let's be honest, most business owners are not leading. They're juggling, firefighting, and stretched so thin trying to keep the business afloat that leadership feels like something that happens later, when there's more time, more people and more structure.

The problem — and the truth — is ... that time never comes.

And here's the biggest truth of all.

True leadership is not about titles or headcounts — it's about authenticity, vision and building real connections with your team. It's about stepping up, setting the tone and creating a culture where people don't just work *for* you but *with* you — because they believe in what you're building.

Yet for so many business owners, this is the part no one prepares them for.

You started a business because you're good at what you do. You built something, gained momentum, and then suddenly you weren't just doing your job anymore, you were managing people … leading people.

No one handed you a playbook on how to navigate team dynamics, set expectations, hold people accountable and get the best out of your team while also keeping the business moving forward.

So you do what most business owners do.

You keep everything on your own shoulders. You hustle harder and micromanage because it feels like the only way to get things done properly, and then you stay in the weeds, because stepping back feels like losing control.

But that's not leadership. That, my friend, is survival mode.

And it's exhausting. I know from painful lived experience exactly how it feels.

That's why *Take Charge* is such a powerful book. Because it cuts through the noise and gets to the heart of what leadership really looks like when you're running a business in the real world.

This book isn't about high-level theories or abstract corporate strategies. It's a practical, no-nonsense guide for small business owners who want to lead with passion and confidence — without the overwhelm.

Claudia's written the leadership book that every small business owner needs — a step-by-step, real-world approach to building a team that works, leading with clarity, and creating a business that *doesn't rely on you to function*.

In *Take Charge*, you will learn how to:

- step out of firefighting mode and into clear, confident leadership so you can stop reacting and start leading;
- build a team that takes ownership, so you don't have to micromanage every detail;
- transform chaotic team dynamics into a culture of trust, accountability and high performance; and
- lead with vision and strategy so your business doesn't just survive — it grows and thrives.

Because here's another truth I know for sure: your business will only grow as fast as you do.

- If you don't step up as a leader, your team won't step up either.
- If you don't create clarity, your business will stay chaotic.
- If you don't shift from *doing everything* to leading strategically, you will always be the bottleneck.

But here's the good news: you don't need to figure this out alone. Claudia has done the work, gathered the knowledge and laid it all out for you in this book.

So take a breath, open your mind, then turn the page and get ready to lead in a way that changes *everything*.

Your business is waiting for the leader you are about to become.

Let's go.

Claire Brumby

In *Take Charge*, you will learn how to:

- step out of firefighting mode and into clear, confident leadership so you can stop reacting and start leading;
- build a team that takes ownership, so you don't have to micromanage every detail;
- transform chaotic team dynamics into a culture of trust, accountability and high performance; and
- lead with vision and strategy so your business doesn't just survive — it grows and thrives.

Because here's another truth I know for sure: your business will only grow as fast as you do.

- If you don't step up as a leader, your team won't step up either.
- If you don't create clarity, your business will stay chaotic.
- If you don't shift from *doing everything* to leading strategically, you will always be the bottleneck.

But here's the good news: you don't need to figure this out alone. Claudia has done the work, gathered the knowledge and laid it all out for you in this book.

So take a breath, open your mind, then turn the page and get ready to lead in a way that changes *everything*.

Your business is waiting for the leader you are about to become.

Let's go.

Claire Brumby

Introduction

When I first started writing this book, I thought it was about helping bosses become better leaders for their teams. And it is — but if I'm honest (and I always try to be), it started as something much more personal. I had just left a job where I felt I could have made a real difference — but my boss made it impossible. They weren't great at managing people or creating a positive culture, and our relationship eventually became unworkable. Now, I'm not saying it was all their fault. I have a very strong sense of what is right and wrong, and I don't shy away from speaking up when something crosses a line. But there were moments in that workplace — public put-downs, casual sexism and outdated attitudes — that left me questioning my place, my value and even my own confidence.

I didn't realise it at the time, but the environment was chipping away at me. I started to doubt myself, thinking maybe I wasn't cut out for the job or that I needed to 'toughen up'. After one particularly demoralising meeting, I filled four entire journal pages with the affirmation 'I am enough'. And that was when I knew something had to change — not just for me, but for anyone who has ever felt undervalued, overlooked or outright mistreated at work. Leaving that job led to another *aha* moment: there are too many workplaces where talented, passionate people are wasted because their leaders don't know how to bring out the best in them. And I wasn't alone in this experience. So many people I spoke to — friends, family, colleagues — shared similar stories of being ignored or micromanaged or feeling like their contributions didn't matter. It broke my heart to think of the untapped potential sitting dormant in workplaces around the world.

As an employee, I used to think bosses were either 'good' or 'bad'. I didn't think much about the person behind the title — their struggles, their doubts or the pressures they faced. But that perspective changed when I was promoted to manager in one of my roles. Suddenly I was responsible for a team, expected to make decisions and get everything right. It was overwhelming, and I often wondered if I was doing enough or if I was even the right person for the job. Years later, as a business coach working with small and medium-sized business owners, I discovered I wasn't alone in feeling this way. Almost every single one of them worries they are falling short. They're not just trying to lead a team, they're also wearing multiple hats — strategist, problem-solver and decision-maker — often without the resources or support of a larger company.

Not just the intention behind the book but even the title has been a journey. Originally the title was geared towards bosses who wanted to manage their staff better to improve retention. But over time it evolved into what you now hold in your hands: *Take Charge*. I realised the original title was too focused on the functional aspects of being a boss — it lacked focus on the person *behind* the role. I wanted a title that spoke first to the person holding the role. Someone who is — just like their team — first and foremost *human* and who deserves the same understanding and grace as the people they manage.

Too often that gets overlooked. Being a boss can be a tough and isolating job: you often don't have anyone to turn to with your questions or worries, your team is naturally more distant from you than they are from their peers, and the weight of responsibility you carry can feel enormous. That was why I needed a title that speaks to you first — a title that says, 'You've got this!' For me, *Take Charge* does exactly that. It shifts the focus away from the role itself and onto the person behind it. It says, 'This book is about you, but it will require you to take the first step. Being in charge isn't automatic — your team needs to see you step into that role. Deep down you know you have it in you to be the perfect boss for a great team that loves showing up and that delivers results. Now it is time to become that leader.' I know that's a lot to read into a title, but that was the thought behind it, at least from my perspective.

You might wonder what makes me the right person to write this book. Fair question! Let me share a little about myself. My journey has been anything but linear: I hold a business degree and have worked in marketing, operations, sales and project management across industries like renewable energy, fashion, professional services and tech. But wherever I worked, one thing remained constant: I had a knack for bringing people together, uncovering their strengths and helping them work as a team — whether it was starting and running my own dance group at age 14, organising book clubs or managing corporate departments. It is just what I do naturally. More than that, I know what it feels like to be mismanaged, overlooked and undervalued. I have seen the damage caused by toxic workplaces, cliquey cultures and poor leadership. I have felt the frustration of seeing great people lose their spark because no one recognised what they were truly capable of.

But I have also seen the incredible transformations that happen when teams are led with care, respect and purpose. That belief — that workplaces can be better, that bosses can be both human and effective, and that together we can change lives — drives everything I do. It is what inspired me to start The Business Fabrik, a consultancy dedicated to helping business owners create workplaces where teams flourish. It is also what inspired me to write this book. I am determined to change the world, one workplace at a time. I believe that when leaders create great workplaces, it doesn't just improve the business — it cascades out into families, communities and beyond. My hope is that you, the reader, share this vision and will join me in making it a reality. Together we can create workplaces that inspire, empower and bring out the best in everyone.

This isn't a book about bashing bad managers or glorifying employees at the expense of their leader. It's about helping you create an environment where everyone — yourself included — can show up as their best self. It is about building a team culture where trust and collaboration replace micromanagement and frustration. If you've ever felt you are 'winging it' as a leader or if you've ever wondered how to get the most out of your team without burning yourself out, this book is for you. It's for the business owner who knows they have untapped potential in their team and wants to unlock it. It's for the boss who wants to build something bigger than themselves but isn't sure how to get there.

I know you already have a lot on your plate, and I know running a business can sometimes feel like a lonely job. But I also know that you have what it takes to make a difference — not just in your business but in the lives of the people who work for you. The fact that you have picked up this book tells me you are ready to understand how you can make a difference.

Where are we?

Before we dive into the nitty-gritty of how to take charge and feel more confident in your role as a leader, let's take a second to understand the challenges that have brought us to this point. You never planned to be a leader, yet here you are — running a business, managing a team and trying to figure out how to get the best out of your people while keeping everything else afloat. No one handed you a leadership manual when you started this journey and chances are, you've had to figure things out as you go. But here's the reality: if you don't get this part right, your best people won't stick around.

We can talk about leadership strategies, but unless we understand why employees leave in the first place, we'll only ever be treating the symptoms — not the root cause. You might assume that the number one reason people leave is money, right? Wrong! Of course, fair pay and benefits matter, but only 16% of US employees,[1] for example, who left their job in 2023 said low pay was their primary reason for leaving. That means a staggering 84% left for reasons beyond their pay cheque.

So what are those reasons? When you think about it, none of them should come as a surprise: one of the most significant factors is a lack of advancement opportunities. Another key issue is the quality of leadership (12%). Relocation accounted for 10% of departures, followed by personal reasons (9%). Other reasons included unrealistic job expectations (7%), boredom or lack of interest in their role (6%), feeling disrespected (4%) and poor work—life balance (3%). As interesting as these numbers are, it's important to note that the survey participants were only allowed to give one primary reason for leaving, but for most people it is rarely just one thing. What all of this tells us is that employees are looking for more than a pay cheque: they want to feel like their work matters. They want to see a future in the company and work in an environment that values them as people, not just cogs in a machine. When those needs aren't met, they leave — or worse, they stay but disengage entirely.

Whether they are physically walking out the door or disengaging, the end result is usually the same: low engagement, poor productivity and frustration on all sides. Gallup's latest *State of the Global Workplace* report[2] showed some sobering statistics: 50% of workers worldwide are ready to leave their job at any moment, and only one in four would recommend their employer to others. Employee loyalty is at an all-time low, and ignoring these facts as a boss and telling yourself that your business will be okay is a dangerous gamble.

Here's where it gets even more concerning: globally, only 21% of employees are genuinely engaged in their work. Let that sink in for a moment. If you have a team of ten people, chances are only two of them are excited to show up each morning. The rest? They are either doing the bare minimum or have mentally checked out altogether — a phenomenon now widely referred to as 'quiet quitting'. For many, work has become something they endure rather than enjoy. This has become particularly true since the COVID-19 pandemic; the shift to remote work gave people the time and space to re-evaluate their priorities, and many realised life isn't all about work. They are no longer willing to go above and beyond unless they feel genuinely appreciated.

For business owners, this presents a massive problem. Disengaged employees are less productive, more likely to call in sick and prone to making mistakes or leaving. Replacing staff isn't cheap either — it can cost anything from six to nine months of an employee's salary to find, onboard and train someone new. Even then, it can take up to 28 weeks for a new hire to reach full productivity. When you combine these individual challenges with the broader realities of running a small business, the scale of the problem becomes obvious.

Small and medium-sized enterprises (SMEs) make up over 90% of businesses worldwide and employ more than 50% of the global workforce. In the UK alone, SMEs account for 99% of all businesses and employ about 60% of private-sector workers. As the backbone of the economy, the success of SMEs is critical — but they face unique challenges larger organisations don't. Unlike big corporations, small business owners often wear multiple hats. They are not just the boss; they are also the strategist, the planner, the problem-solver and sometimes even the IT department. When you're juggling so many roles, it's easy to feel overwhelmed by the task of motivating a team that seems increasingly hard to connect with. You might find yourself wondering: how do you re-engage a team that feels disconnected? How do you reignite your own passion when so much of your energy is spent trying to motivate others?

The solution is not to accept disengagement as the new norm, and it's certainly not to endlessly replace staff in the hope that the next hire will be different. The answer lies in creating a workplace where people genuinely want to be — a place that doesn't fill them with dread on a Sunday night but that they are happy to get out of bed for. This book is your guide to making that happen. If you want your team to be excited about their work, to proudly tell their friends and family about where they work and give their best every day, it starts here — with you.

Building an inspiring team culture isn't about waving a magic wand or relying on one single ingredient. It's like a recipe for the perfect dish — it needs the right balance of components:

- the right organisational structure
- for the right people
- in the right roles
- working towards a shared goal
- playing by the same rules.

Sounds complicated? It doesn't have to be. By picking up this book, you've already taken the first step towards building a great team, creating happier employees, increasing productivity and giving yourself more freedom as the business owner. Will it be easy? Not always. Change never is! This book will walk you through the process step by step, but the real work — on yourself, on your goals, on your team — is up to you. There will be tough conversations to be had, resistance to deal with and moments when you might doubt yourself or the journey. But trust me, if you stick with it, the rewards will be worth it. Imagine a team that shows up excited to work every day. They know exactly what is expected of them and why. They take pride in being part of something bigger. They are walking advertisements for your business. Your customers will notice a difference, your company will blossom and you will finally be able to breathe. You will trust your team, take time off without worrying and make yourself a priority again.

How to read this book

If you've made it this far, congratulations — you're already one step closer to building the team and business you've always dreamed of. This book isn't just something to read — it is something to *do*. It's a guide, a roadmap and, hopefully, a source of encouragement when things feel hard. This is an activity-based book, designed to guide you through practical exercises that help you better understand yourself, your leadership style and your team.

To get the most out of the exercises, I recommend a dedicated notebook or journal to capture your thoughts and progress. You will also find accompanying documents and templates available for download at www.takecharge-thebook.com, designed to help you implement the strategies and tools in real time. Details on accessing these resources are provided in this book, so be sure to have them handy as you go. Find a space where you can work on these exercises without distractions — somewhere that puts you in a positive and focused frame of mind. Treat this as your time to reflect, plan and grow — both as a boss and as an individual.

The structure of the book is simple and intentional and is based on my BOSS method, divided into four main sections:

1. **Be the Boss Your Business Needs:** A section focusing on you — your mindset, your confidence and the kind of leader your business needs you to be. Leadership starts with showing up as the best version of yourself, and this is where we will begin.
2. **Organise the Ideal:** Here we will create a vision for your business. We will map out the ideal structure, define roles and set clear goals to create the foundation for a strong team.
3. **Survey the Current Reality:** Take a hard look at where things stand right now, assess your team's strengths, weaknesses and engagement levels and figure out who is in the right role — and who might not be.
4. **Strategise and Make It Happen:** Finally we will bring it all together, where your team buys into your vision, shared values are developed and you create an intentional culture.

At the end of every chapter, you will find BOSS facts — key principles designed to reinforce the chapter's core lessons and help you take immediate action. These aren't just reminders; they are practical, bite-sized takeaways to keep you grounded and focused as you apply what you have learned. Think of them as your leadership compass, providing clarity and direction when challenges arise. Whether you are revisiting them for inspiration or using them to guide a tough decision, the BOSS facts are there to support you throughout your journey to building a motivated team.

The chapters are short on purpose, so you can work through them at your own pace, whether that's one chapter at a time or in bigger chunks. I recommend following the process chapter by chapter for best results. Each step builds on the last, and skipping ahead might mean missing crucial parts of the journey. Don't rush, and don't worry if things feel overwhelming at first. The goal is progress, not perfection. Throughout the book, you'll find practical exercises, tools and strategies designed to help you take immediate action. Use them. Ideas are great, but action is what creates real change. Pause when you need to. Revisit chapters as things evolve. This is not a 'do it once and be done with it' kind of process — it's a journey, and I will be with you every step of the way. Trust the process, be bold and put your bossy pants on — you're already halfway there.

By the time you finish this book, you will have everything you need to build a team that loves showing up to work — and a business you are proud to lead. But it starts with you. It starts with committing to this process and showing up for your team and yourself.

You've got this. Let's get to work.

1. Be the Boss Your Business Needs

Before we dive into the 'how to' of transforming your existing team, we need to look at something much more important for long-term success — the person in charge and at the helm of it all: you. Without you, there would be no business. Without you, no one would have their job. Without you, your customers would need to find help elsewhere. You might have heard the saying 'the fish stinks from the head' — whether you like it or not, you are the head of the fish. If you stink, the whole fish — your team — stinks. If you are scented, well cared for and kept refrigerated, so is the rest of your company.

Okay, okay, I obviously cannot condone putting team members in the fridge or spraying them with perfume, but you get my point. You are the person at the front; you set the tempo, the direction and the mood. Unchecked, your values become the company values. If you don't create a culture, you will get the one you tolerate. If you don't know where you're going, if you doubt yourself or the business, if you are lacking energy or have an overall less-than-ideal attitude, so will your team and so will your customers.

Don't believe that your attitude affects the customers your business attracts? Oh, think again, my friend. Let me explain: it starts with the hiring process and the people you hire. Whether you realise it or not, on some level everyone you hire will be similar. Your choices are shaped by unconscious biases, cultural norms and the desire for harmony and predictability within the team. You choose candidates based on their similarities to you (e.g. if they have the same educational background), if they confirm pre-existing beliefs you hold (e.g. of what makes a good employee), if they seem familiar (e.g. they remind you of an existing employee) or even if they fit within a certain gender, age group or ethnicity.

A lot of this happens on a subconscious level. Their looks, what they said and how they said it sparked something inside you that made you hire them. As much as you are trying to tell yourself that you hired them solely on qualifications, chances are, that would be a lie. It's more likely you liked them on an emotional level first and then justified their hiring through the facts afterwards. Little fun fact for you to prove my point: while the average interview takes about 40 minutes, a third of hiring managers admit they know in the first 90 seconds if they are hiring someone or not.[3]

Unless you involved other people in the recruitment process (and genuinely listened to their input), that is true for all your team members, and you're now in charge of a team with, maybe not obviously but on some level, very similar people: maybe they all have the same energy level or the same level of proactivity. Are they maybe all a bit secretive? Or the opposite and they speak their mind all the time, sometimes leading to heated discussions? Do they all think they know best? Do they all have very similar family situations? Are they all outgoing or maybe more introverted? On some level (and that level might not be immediately obvious to you), they will all share some commonalities. That is normal and to be expected; you hired people who made you feel safe. Safe because they didn't seem to threaten your authority. Safe because they seemed easy enough to manage. Safe because they would fit in well with the existing team. You get my point.

Now their values, attitudes and motivations (which are the ones you subconsciously picked in the interview) run your client interactions. They are the people who answer the phone, pack the orders, handle the complaints. An extroverted, grumpy staff member will talk differently to a client than an introverted, positive person will. But it's not just actual client interactions. Think about your website and social media. They include the words that prospects first get to know you by, so they decide which prospects they attract in the first place. Take for example the words 'simple' vs 'efficient' or 'trusted' vs 'proven'. They both mean the same thing but, used in a marketing context, will attract a very different crowd. Who writes the copy for those posts? Your marketing team? Who hired them, then? I think you're getting where I'm going with this; whether you realise it or not, the people you hire set the tone for how your business treats its clients — even with manuals, scripts and the like.

Why am I telling you all this? The culture and reputation of a business are shaped by the people inside it, and a team is shaped by the person who put it together. As a result, your team will always be a 'light' version of yourself; its members share many of the same values, share your attitude to risk and change, their proactiveness (or lack thereof), etc. So to make any sort of lasting change in your business and your team, you will need to start with yourself. You need to up your own game first. If you're in a different frame of mind (more focused, more motivated, etc.), you will hire a different kind of person, and your existing team will take notice if you do or say things differently and will, over time, adapt accordingly.

It might or might not be your fault where your team stands at the moment, but it's absolutely 100% your responsibility to decide where it goes from here. Blaming others keeps you stuck in the past, while taking responsibility shifts your focus to the future — and gives you the power to create it. Responsibility isn't just about accountability; it's also about response-ability — the ability to choose how you respond to the challenges and opportunities around you. Your response shapes your team, your culture and ultimately your results. No matter what you're hoping to build or whose fault you think it is, the first and most critical change is yours to make. That's why this book starts with you: before you lead your team, you first need to lead yourself.

Claudia D **THOMPSON**

Am I a leader? Am I a manager?

The minute you become a boss, it stops being about you and starts being about the people you employ. Being a boss shifts the focus from your personal desires and achievements to the growth and wellbeing of your team. Your success is no longer just measured by profit and turnover but by how well you empower others, how effectively you communicate and how much they enjoy coming to work.

At one point you will have to let other people know in some shape or form what they are expected to do — it's time to lead them. Or is it time to manage them? Let's find out! In today's world, the two words are often used interchangeably, and while a manager can be a great leader and a leader can be a great manager, this is not always the case. Let's look a bit deeper.

'Leadership' and 'being a great leader' are some of the buzzwords of our time; endless books have been written about leadership and what it takes to be a good leader. In fact, the search for leadership titles on Amazon alone reveals over 60,000 results, and with thousands of new books published every year, there is certainly no shortage of material on how to become a successful leader. So is leadership — as the plethora of teaching material suggests — a series of skills you can learn or is it something you must be born with to make it among the greats?

This nature vs nurture debate is at least as old as the concept of leading itself. Both perspectives have plenty of merit and find support through research and expert opinions. A study done by the Center for Creative Leadership revealed that 52% of senior executives believe leadership can be learned, with 19% believing that leaders are born and 29% believing it is a mixture of both.[4] Meanwhile a twin study published in *Leadership Quarterly* found that about 30% of leadership traits could be attributed to genetic factors.[5] There are many more surveys on the topic, and the consensus seems to be that leadership is probably a combination of innate qualities and learned skills.

Many of us have never stopped to reflect on how those qualities (or lack thereof) show up in our own leadership style. You might have never thought about whether you are naturally more inclined to lead or manage — or what that means for your business. Understanding this can be a game-changer for how you approach your role. The truth is, most people love to be led. They love the idea of following someone else's vision and being warmed by their light. Mahatma Gandhi, Martin Luther King Jr, Abraham Lincoln and Nelson Mandela are just some of the leaders in history who painted the image of a world they longed to see so brightly that others couldn't help but want to be part of that world. They didn't set out to rally thousands of people behind their cause. They knew there was a better way of doing things and by speaking up about it, people started taking notice. Over time a whisper turned into a movement that changed the world.

Did those historic leaders ever take lessons in leadership? Although I have to admit I'm not 100% sure, I doubt it. So even though there are plenty of courses, books, workshops, etc. out there, don't feel like you need just one more course to know how to lead your team. The truth is, it once again starts with you. Where are you leading them? What is your picture of a better world? What do you want to be remembered for? Don't worry, you don't need ideas of changing the law, changing the world or an equally lofty vision; you just need an idea of where you want your business to go. This is what we'll look at in Chapter 2.

Note how I didn't say people love to be managed. People love to be led, but they don't love to be managed (or to be told what to do, which is the layperson's definition of 'management'). Your job as a boss becomes a lot easier if you are the leader of your team. Having said that, they will also need a manager. And because there's a clear distinction between leadership and management and they both have their place, the following pages are dedicated to helping you figure out which one of the two comes more naturally to you. If you are the self-deprecating type, please don't worry: one of the two will be more you, I promise. You wouldn't be the owner of a business that employs people if you hadn't done something right (we'll get into exactly what makes you the right person for the job later in this chapter — see: 'Where has my mojo gone?').

So what exactly is the difference between leadership and management? The main difference between the two centres around their focus, approach and responsibilities. Both are crucial for business success — neither is better than the other, and neither makes you a better or worse business person. While the roles can overlap, managers and leaders emphasise different aspects of the organisation. A leader focuses on vision, people and inspiration. They tend to drive long-term change and innovation and motivate their team through a shared sense of purpose. People feel naturally drawn to leaders. They get inspired by them, trust them, listen to them and let them lead the way.

Leaders come in all shapes and sizes; they can be a teacher at school, a colleague, a politician, a nurse, one of your kid's friends, etc. They aren't necessarily the loudest people in the room; they have a clear vision and almost as if by magic can rally people together to support their cause. They usually have a quiet reassurance about them. They know who they are and what they stand for at their core — even if they often don't realise it themselves or haven't made full use of their talents because they haven't found their purpose yet. In the workplace, leaders tend to be great assets to a company; they get stuff done, and their colleagues like them and seek their advice. If the business owner happens to be a leader, it is a recipe for success: they usually build great companies, often with a big purpose; their teams are engaged and are proud to follow their boss's vision.

A manager, by contrast, focuses on execution, processes and efficiency, ensuring the day-to-day operations of the business run smoothly, tasks are completed and goals are met in the short term. The word 'manager' derives from the Italian 'maneggiare', which means 'to handle' or 'to train (horses)' and comes from the Latin word 'manus' for hand. As the name suggests, managers are responsible for handling their employees. They use things like performance reviews, incentives and clear goals to motivate their staff. They make sure everyone knows what to do and how to do it and then hold them accountable to ensure they do the work. Managers tend to be the firefighters in a business.

You need some more examples to bring the point home, I hear you say? No problem. Let's look at some famous movie examples:

For the Fantasy Fan: In Lord of the Rings, Aragorn represents the manager in many ways. He handles the tactical operations, ensures safety, keeps people fed, rallies them for specific battles, and makes sure they are prepared and in the right place. Gandalf, on the other hand, embodies leadership qualities: he sees the bigger picture, inspires others and focuses on guiding Middle Earth towards a greater purpose.

For the Disney Devotee: Mufasa in *The Lion King* is the embodiment of leadership. He inspires respect and admiration and guides others with his vision for the circle of life (cue singing monkey!). After his death, the pride falls apart. Zazu, his loyal adviser bird, is more of a manager; he focuses on details, keeps everyone in line and reports back to Mufasa. He handles the day-to-day operations to make sure the kingdom runs smoothly.

For the Action Addict: James Bond and M. Even though James Bond is on the frontline delivering the work, he is the ultimate leader in the field — he's adaptable, decisive and willing to take risks to complete the mission. He has very strong values and operates with a big-picture focus, trusts his instincts and rallies allies as needed. Bond often inspires loyalty in others. M, on the other hand, is the ultimate firefighter. They are responsible for overseeing operations, managing resources and making strategic decisions that support the mission from behind the scenes. M maintains control, sets boundaries and ensures Bond's actions align with MI6's wider goals. They are practical, detail-oriented and often need to remind Bond of the rules and consequences. Their relationship also beautifully highlights the tension and balance between visionary leadership and structured management — Bond, as leader, thrives on flexibility and pushing limits, while M provides the stability, oversight and strategic thinking needed to keep the mission on course.

While the previous examples showed the dynamic between iconic leaders and managers, the following two examples show the transformative journeys of individuals who had to learn to embrace both roles. These examples show how developing qualities of both leadership and management isn't just beneficial — it is often essential for success.

An example of someone who starts as a manager but learns to lead can be found in *Saving Private Ryan*. Captain Miller begins as a focused manager — he is a capable soldier who executes missions efficiently, ensuring his team follows orders and accomplishes its objectives. However, as the film progresses, Miller is thrust into a situation that requires more than just tactical management. Leading a group of diverse soldiers on a highly emotional mission, he learns to inspire them, connect with their motivations and help them see the bigger picture beyond survival — bringing Private Ryan home to honour the sacrifices of others. His journey shows the transformation from a by-the-book manager to a leader who earns the respect and trust of his team by embodying purpose and humanity.

On the flip side, in *The Avengers*, Tony Stark (aka Iron Man) begins as a natural leader — charismatic, visionary, bold. He is great at inspiring people and coming up with visionary ideas. However, his individualistic style creates tension in a team setting. Over time, he learns to manage — working with others, balancing egos and building trust within the group. Tony's growth reflects the importance of managing details and dynamics alongside leading with vision.

These examples demonstrate how leadership and management complement each other to achieve a common goal and that someone can have and develop attributes of both. I hope they also demonstrate that neither of the two is more important than the other. Yes, the movie is usually named after the leader, but none of the examples above (or any other example you can think of) would have been able to achieve what they did if it weren't for the manager on their side.

Exercise: Leader assessment
10 minutes

Did I mention this is an activity-based book? Well, it's now time for your first exercise. In this one you will determine whether you are naturally more of a leader or a manager. Over the following pages you will find a list of attributes traditionally associated with either leadership or management. For each attribute, read the 'I' statements underneath and rate yourself on a scale of 1 to 5, where 1 means 'nope, not me' and 5 means 'I am perfect at this'.

At the end of the exercise, add your points together to calculate your total score out of 125 for both leadership and management. For all the exercises in this book, please be honest with yourself. Don't answer the questions with what you wish to be true, but instead reflect on past feedback from friends, family and employees, as well as your own experiences.

Vision and strategy

I articulate a clear and compelling vision for the future of the business.	
I align team goals with the long-term objectives of the organisation.	
I think strategically about the big picture and long-term success.	
I effectively balance innovation with realistic goal setting.	
I anticipate challenges and plan strategically to address them.	

Inspiration and motivation

I inspire my team by communicating purpose and meaning in their work.	
I celebrate individual and team successes regularly.	
I encourage creativity and new ideas within the team.	
I create an environment where people feel motivated to do their best.	
I take an active role in developing team members' potential.	

Adaptability, decisiveness and resilience

I stay focused and calm in periods of uncertainty or change.	
I make timely decisions, even in complex situations.	
I adapt my leadership approach to suit different team needs.	
I effectively navigate setbacks and maintain team morale.	
I maintain a positive outlook and help my team stay motivated during challenges.	

Communication skills and relationship building

I communicate openly and authentically with my team.	
I actively listen to team members' concerns and ideas.	
I build trust by being transparent and dependable.	
I ensure every team member feels valued and included.	
I resolve conflicts constructively and in a timely manner.	

Humility and empathy

I acknowledge and learn from my mistakes.	
I seek feedback from my team to improve my leadership.	
I show empathy by understanding and addressing team members' concerns.	
I value the perspectives and contributions of every team member.	
I prioritise the team's success over personal recognition.	

Leader score: /125

Exercise: Manager assessment
10 minutes

Planning and organisation

I set clear, actionable goals for the team to achieve.	
I create structured and detailed plans to meet objectives.	
I manage time effectively to balance priorities.	
I anticipate and prepare for potential risks to our plans.	
I ensure resources are allocated efficiently.	

Execution and monitoring

I regularly monitor the team's progress toward goals.	
I take corrective action promptly when projects deviate from plans.	
I ensure high quality standards are met for all deliverables.	
I follow through on plans and commitments consistently.	
I celebrate milestones to keep the team motivated.	

Problem-solving

I proactively address challenges that arise during projects.	
I think critically and creatively to find effective solutions.	
I analyse data and feedback before making decisions.	
I involve the right people to solve complex issues.	
I resolve bottlenecks without compromising deadlines or quality.	

Accountability and feedback

I hold team members accountable for their responsibilities.	
I address underperformance promptly and constructively.	
I provide regular and specific feedback to help team members improve.	
I ask for and act on feedback from my team to enhance performance.	
I recognise team members for their contributions and efforts.	

Exercise: Manager assessment
10 minutes

Planning and organisation

I set clear, actionable goals for the team to achieve.	
I create structured and detailed plans to meet objectives.	
I manage time effectively to balance priorities.	
I anticipate and prepare for potential risks to our plans.	
I ensure resources are allocated efficiently.	

Execution and monitoring

I regularly monitor the team's progress toward goals.	
I take corrective action promptly when projects deviate from plans.	
I ensure high quality standards are met for all deliverables.	
I follow through on plans and commitments consistently.	
I celebrate milestones to keep the team motivated.	

Problem-solving

I proactively address challenges that arise during projects.
I think critically and creatively to find effective solutions.
I analyse data and feedback before making decisions.
I involve the right people to solve complex issues.
I resolve bottlenecks without compromising deadlines or quality.

Accountability and feedback

I hold team members accountable for their responsibilities.
I address underperformance promptly and constructively.
I provide regular and specific feedback to help team members improve.
I ask for and act on feedback from my team to enhance performance.
I recognise team members for their contributions and efforts.

Delegation, communication and clarity

I delegate tasks based on individual strengths and expertise.	
I ensure every team member understands their roles and responsibilities.	
I provide clear instructions and expectations for tasks and projects.	
I encourage open communication about progress and challenges.	
I balance delegation with providing support when needed.	

Manager score: /125

Once you've completed the exercise, it's time to calculate your scores. Add up your ratings for the leadership statements and the manager statements to get your respective totals. Each category has a maximum score of 125. Your totals will give you an insight into where your natural strengths lie. A higher leadership total indicates you naturally excel in areas like vision, inspiration and motivation, while a higher management total suggests strong skills in planning, execution and accountability.

Take a moment to reflect on your results. Think about how they align with feedback you've received from others or patterns you have noticed in your own behaviour. This isn't about achieving perfection in every area but understanding where you shine and where you can grow.

How did you do? Which one of the two spoke more to you? Did you realise there are more areas to consider than you previously thought? Even if you didn't score as highly as you would have hoped, hopefully this exercise has given you an idea about which areas you could look at improving. The great news is: you now have a starting point and you get to choose how you deal with the result. Say you realise inspiration is your challenging area, you can then find help on how to inspire others and start to get better at it, or if you found that processes are practically non-existent in your business, you can start learning and working on that.

When you recognise that some areas could (and probably should) be improved and you *choose* (remember, we talked about response-ability earlier) to take action, you open the door to growth and transformation. The real question is: do you want to turn your staff into a trusted team that loves working together? Do you want to lead a business that is not only more profitable but also more fulfilling to run? Change and growth often mean stepping outside your comfort zone, but the rewards are so worth it. If you're not quite ready to embrace the challenge, that's okay too. Growth happens when we're ready for it, and this book will be here for you when the time feels right. For now, take this as a moment to reflect, and when you're ready to take the next step, this will be your guide.

To be great, a business needs both — leadership and management. You will need to be the leader when it comes to inspiring your team, setting the vision and making high-level decisions. Management skills are required to execute plans, optimise processes and maintain accountability. If you have found out in the previous exercise that you're clearly more on one of the two sides, you might want to look into finding someone in your team or recruiting someone to complement your skillset. If you're more naturally a manager, identify the natural leaders in your team and get them involved more. If you're a natural leader, it might be useful to introduce a management team or a manager to run the day-to-day operations. We will look at how to find and promote suitable people in Chapters 3 and 4.

Where has my mojo gone?

A lot of content is available for how to motivate your team as a boss, but not many people talk about what happens if the boss themselves needs a boost. The truth is, one major reason why teams lack motivation is because their boss has lost their mojo. Maybe you recognise yourself a little bit in this. Do you find yourself spending less and less time doing the things you enjoy? Are the competition or market conditions getting to you? Are things harder than you thought? There are endless reasons why you might not be your original perky self, and they are all valid. You are human, after all. And because it's such a common occurrence and affects so many businesses, this chapter is dedicated to rekindling your motivation, or, if you don't feel you are lacking it, it will give you a nice confidence boost, and we can all do with that.

Let's spend a moment to look back to when you started your business. What made you say yes? What made you kick all concerns into the wind to start against all the odds? What did you have in mind for its future? If you're like most business owners, you didn't exactly have a plan in mind but more a rough idea for a better life. Maybe you saw the chance to do better, to do business in a way that hadn't been done before — an idea in your head that was impossible to ignore. Or did you just want to fix an existing problem? You saw a need and you went in to do it better?

If you've just been nodding along during that last paragraph, it means you started your business from a personal conviction — highly motivated and enthusiastic, which are two crucial attributes when it comes to starting and growing a business. Unfortunately, those two also easily get lost when the day-to-day frustrations become so many that you lose sight of the 'fun' bits in your business — the bits that you enjoy and that made you start in the first place. When the annoying things make up most of your day, the daily grind becomes just that, and you feel less and less excited to go to work in the morning.

Depending on your personality type, skillset and interests, those annoyances come from different things: having to figure out the nitty-gritty of a new system when you are more of a big picture person, having people interrupt your daily workflow when you feel they should know the answers already, accounting, bookkeeping, stockkeeping — there's an endless list of tasks that can rob you of your enthusiasm. And your enthusiasm is the most important asset you have. It is what will get your team and business through sticky patches, it is what will make you take risks to grow your business, it is what creates new ideas, attracts new customers, etc. It is worth protecting. In fact, you don't just need to protect it, you need to build an impregnable fortress around it, defend it with everything you have. If you lose it, it affects not just your business, it affects your whole life. If you're no longer excited to go to work, it becomes a drag. You are less inclined to speak to your team, and your team will slowly lose their enthusiasm, making you more annoyed because it's harder to motivate them. Eventually that irritation may follow you into your personal life, leading to arguments at home, which can in turn lead to more irritation in the office and so on.

Let's treat that enthusiasm of yours like the Olympic flame. The Olympic flame is ignited in a sacred ceremony that connects the modern Games to their ancient roots. Just like your business idea, this ceremony marks the birth of a vision. Once lit, the Olympic torch then travels across continents, protected against wind, rain and other elements to ensure it stays lit. It is kept burning continuously from its ignition until the end of the Games. It is the ultimate symbol of resilience, endurance, commitment and unwavering spirit.

Did you know that in the lighting ceremony, if clouds prevent the use of the parabolic mirror to light the flame with sunlight, they have a backup flame that was lit during one of the dress rehearsals? There are also multiple copies of the flame that travel alongside the main torch relay or are maintained in backup locations in case the torch or Olympic cauldron is accidentally extinguished. You don't have a backup flame for your enthusiasm, so it's even more important to look after what you've got.

Whether your personal Olympic flame is still as bright as it once was or whether it lately resembles more of a flickering candle struggling to stay alight, it reflects on your business. To energise others, you must first re-energise yourself. Your team will always reflect you and your actions. If you're enthusiastic, they will be. If you are bored, frustrated, just firefighting, stuck in the daily grind, they will be. They have the prerogative to go home at the end of the day and not worry any more about your business until the following day, while you are always 'on' You don't get to choose when to not care about the business. So isn't it worth making sure you're as enthusiastic as possible? Yes, it is! Let the following exercise help you — not just to regain your mojo but also to set you up for what else is to follow in the later chapters of this book.

Exercise: Reignite and reflect
60 minutes

Find a quiet place where you won't be disturbed to spend some time with the questions on the following pages. It's crucial to set that time aside and make sure you won't get interrupted. For this exercise to work at its best, it's important to get in the zone and go deep. You're laying the foundations for the future of your business here, so if you find yourself looking for reasons and excuses why you can't do it or do it half-heartedly, know that this is your brain at work trying to keep you safe and avoid discomfort!

Next to each topic you will find a dedicated time allocation. Stay with the questions for the whole time assigned, even if you think you are finished. The best answers will come to you *after* you think you've already found them all. Once you're ready to go, don't overthink it, and write whatever comes to mind. Don't judge the answers. Don't think about whether they are right or wrong or whether they even make sense. This is your time, your space, your answers — no judgement here. So set your 15-minute timer and off you go.

Reflect on your why
15 minutes

What excited you about your business idea?

What problems were you passionate about solving?

What goals did you set out to achieve?

_____

_____

_____

_____

_____

_____

_____

_____

_____

Revisit your successes
15 minutes

List all the milestones and successes you or your business have achieved since you started. Consider:

- key achievements (even the small wins!),
- positive feedback from customers and clients,
- challenges you overcame that made you stronger,
- personal growth you have experienced as a business owner, and
- how many team members have an income thanks to your business.

Identify why you are the right person for the job
15 minutes

Reflect on your unique strengths, skills and qualities that make you the right person to lead this business. Include:

- your expertise and experience in the industry,
- personal attributes that have contributed to your success (e.g. resilience, creativity, leadership, etc.),
- specific skills you have developed that are crucial for your business, and
- any unique perspective or approach you bring to your business that differentiates you from others.

Highlight what's great about your business
15 minutes

List all the things that make your business special. This could include:

- unique products or services you offer,
- exceptional customer services or client relationships,*
- the positive impact your business has on the community, and
- innovative practices, technologies or approaches.

* Be specific with this one. What makes you better than your competitor in the field? 'Great customer service' should be a given for any business and isn't usually what makes people buy from you. What makes you better? How do you go the extra mile? If you struggle to come up with answers to this question, consider surveying your existing customers to find out why they buy from you and not the competition.

_____

_____

_____

_____

_____

_____

Great job! You just reconnected with the reasons why you started your business and the progress you've already achieved. This reflection helps you confirm why you are exactly the right person to lead your business forward and make it a company people are proud to work for.

If you're looking for more ways to stay motivated as a business owner, the following tips might offer exactly the boost you need.

Get interested

Interest and enthusiasm are contagious — not only to others but also to yourself. You can boost your motivation by actively getting interested in the goals you want to achieve and the tasks you will need do to get there. As David J. Schwartz advises in his bestselling book *The Magic of Thinking Big*, just dig in. Learn more about the things you want to achieve, because increased knowledge and understanding can spark greater interest, which in turn leads to higher motivation. So get interested. Look into the things you want to achieve and learn more about them. Want to be listed on the FTSE100? Find out what that means. Want to introduce a new Customer Relationship Management (CRM) system? Compare available solutions. Want to introduce tools that measure your business's diversity, equity and inclusion efforts (DEI)? Read up on them. Having something to learn and explore will fire up your enthusiasm.

Surround yourself with the right people

You are the sum of the five people you spend the most time with — a concept first popularised by Jim Rohn. It suggests the people we surround ourselves with greatly influence our thoughts and behaviours and eventually shape who we become. This concept has been scientifically proven numerous times (look up 'neural synchronisation' if you need the details). Your spouse or the people you live with have the strongest influence on you (fun fact: that's why a lot of couples tend to look alike if they've been together long enough).

If you are lacking motivation, look at the people around you. How do they approach life? What is their attitude? Sometimes it's the people who love us the most that unknowingly hold us back. I'm not saying you should leave your spouse or change your circle of friends. I am saying ensure you're aware of their influence and make every effort to add to your schedule some time with people who have already achieved what you want to achieve or have at least got a great attitude. Join networking groups, mastermind sessions or appropriate online forums to connect you with the right people.

Invest in self-care

Burnout is real and could be the reason for a lack of motivation: constantly trying to burn the candle at both ends or feeling overwhelmed can impact passion. Make sure you're setting boundaries to avoid overworking. Step away from the business regularly to recharge. You can't build an empire if you're running on empty. Dedicate time to exercise and time for your family, hobbies or whatever else you need for 'you time'.

Don't just do the things other people do; listen to your own advice and do what fuels you. If it's a weekend alone in a hut in a forest, so be it. If it's an evening in the fancy restaurant in town, do that. If it's a visit to the spa with all the treatments available, do that. If it means spending a childfree weekend with your spouse, find someone to look after the kids and do it. Look after yourself — especially if you feel you don't deserve it or haven't earned it yet. Your mood, energy and attitude ripple through the team, so it's essential to manage your wellbeing. Showing up with a positive and resilient mindset inspires others to bring their best selves to work.

Consider mentorship or coaching

When we are too deep in our own worries, we can lose perspective, and a set of outsider eyes can help identify changes, see things you might have missed or offer advice on handling the more draining aspects to spark your excitement again. Just like a business therapist, a coach will listen to you and use their experience to navigate you through the jungle and help you with that Olympic flame.

Build-a-boss

One of the best things about reading or listening to personal development books is that you get to reinvent yourself to a degree. You get inspired by what you read and incorporate a little something of what you learned into your daily life and make it your new reality. It's no different for a book about leading a team like the one you're holding right now. You get to take a moment and decide what kind of leader you want to be.

Yes, being an outgoing, confident leader who seemingly always knows the right thing to say, finds it easy to build a rapport with people and sees how things can be improved comes more naturally to some. Maybe they had parents who believed in them when yours didn't, went to a better school than you, grew up in a better neighbourhood or had a more inspiring leader — we can play this game forever. You could forever assume that other people can do what you can't or (and this is my preferred method) you decide (yes, decide!) that your past is what shaped you to this point and you are in charge of how your story continues from here.

You create the future that awaits you. You are no longer just a victim of circumstances; you shape your life. Even Abraham Lincoln knew almost two hundred years ago that 'The best way to predict the future is to create it'. Nobody but you can decide how your story (and your business) continues from here. Yet most of us have no idea where we want to go or what we want to achieve and therefore never even get into a position where we can prove ourselves or find out how close we can get to our full potential. We're playing it safe, and we're meant to. Your brain is designed that way. It's designed to talk you out of new ideas that it deems risky. It does this by convincing you that you aren't good enough anyway, so you might as well not bother. For now, let's thank our brain for its fantastic work and tell it that we are just going to try and see how far we can go anyway.

Through the last exercise, you should have a good idea about your current reality and starting point regarding management and leadership and which areas offer the most room for improvement. Now we know where you currently are, it's time to shift our focus towards where you want to be: your new and improved you — the future you who runs an incredibly successful business with the help of a team of proud ambassadors working towards a vision that has the potential to change the world if you wish.

Think about what that version of you needs to look like. What do they wear? What do they say? How do they carry themselves? What do the team and customers say about them?

Just between you and me, do you think current you has everything it takes to make that happen? Does current you know who to hire to take the business to the next level? Has current you got the right boundaries in place to get what you want? Does current you know how to delegate effectively?

Chances are, you just had to admit that there might be a thing or two that you could work on to achieve your long-term vision. The good news is that *this* is your chance to create the future version of yourself that can do all these cool things. You get to sculpt them like Michelangelo sculpted the David statue, with a clear vision in mind, then carving and chiselling off layer by layer by layer. It took Michelangelo three years to complete the David sculpture. Nobody can say how long it will take you or when you will even be 'finished', but to get anywhere, the first thing is to get started and to know where you're going. And that's what we're doing right now.

On www.takecharge-thebook.com you can find a template for your future boss manifesto, your declaration about who you are as the owner of your business, and some prompt questions to help you cover all areas of leadership and management. This is your ticket to shaping the future you. The manifesto is made up of positive affirmations — phrases for you to say to yourself aloud or in your head. All you need to do is repeat those phrases to yourself every morning and every evening. It also won't hurt to have them written down somewhere so you have a visual reminder.

To make them stick and create lasting, long-term changes to the way you think and feel, it requires regular practice. When you first tell yourself these things, you will feel like a fraud and like you're lying to yourself, but over time, if you keep at it consistently, you'll find that your attitude begins to shift and you are moving more and more into the ideal boss image that you've painted in your manifesto.

And yes, even though it might sound very woo woo, there is science behind this — Claude Steele's self-affirmation theory, which he first introduced in 1988. There is even MRI evidence suggesting that certain neural pathways are created or improved when people practise self-affirmations regularly. To be specific, your ventromedial prefrontal cortex, the part of your brain involved in positive valuation and self-related information processing, becomes more active.[6] If you want more proof, there are many examples of empirical studies further suggesting that positive affirmations can be very beneficial. Just look it up.

We all have a story inside us that we tell ourselves, and no matter what that story is, we will always find proof that we are right. By writing down what kind of boss you want to be, you're writing a new story. Over time and with regular practice, your self-identity will look for ways to not only say these things to yourself but to also follow up with actions that are consistent with what you're saying. So whatever you tell yourself, make sure you're saying things that move you towards the person you want to be and don't keep you repeating the same experiences that brought you where you are today in the first place.

It's not just about sweet talking

As you've seen in this chapter, communication is an important skill for both leaders and managers. And if you're still not entirely convinced about the crucial role communication plays in the workplace, maybe the following statistics will convince you:

- 97% of workers say communication impacts their task efficacy on a daily basis.
- 85% of employees report feeling more motivated when management offers regular updates on company news.
- Effective team communication and collaboration increase employee retention by 4.5 times.[7]
- 86% of employees cite a lack of effective collaboration and communication as the main cause of workplace failures.[8]
- Poor communication in the workplace reportedly accounts for a loss of 7.47 hours per employee per week. For an average US worker earning a salary of $66,976, that amounts to $12,506 per employee per year in sunk costs. For the UK and US markets, these losses are estimated to be around $37 billion a year.[7]

These statistics might make even the most cynical reader reconsider the role communication plays in their business. Communication is one of those skills that we tend to take for granted. It's just something we do, and 'great communication skills' is listed on almost every job application, but let's get real: what does that actually mean? Social media might make you think communication is all about public speaking or always knowing the perfect thing to say. But at its core, communication is simply an exchange of messages — both sending and receiving information. Here's the thing: everyone talks about the 'sending' part, but the 'receiving' part is often neglected. Remember, you have two ears and one mouth for a reason. Even nature is telling you to listen twice as much as you speak.

Communication: The foundation of trust

Trust is the bedrock of any successful team, and it is built (and broken) through communication. When bosses communicate openly, honestly and consistently, it creates a culture where employees know they can trust their superior and they feel secure and valued. It's not just about sharing good news or updates, it's also about being transparent about challenges, admitting mistakes and inviting input. In fact, research conducted by Brosix in 2023 shows that 80% of employees see communication as the number one factor that inspires trust between them and their company.[10] Yet despite this, 58% of employees say they trust strangers more than their own boss,[11] and 81% don't trust their boss to tell the truth.[12]

These numbers are shocking, but they highlight one important truth: without genuine communication, there can be no trust. When trust is lacking, employees are less likely to share ideas, raise concerns or go the extra mile. The natural power imbalance between employees and their boss means that, as the boss, you must work even harder to show your team they can trust you, their jobs are safe and you have their best interests at heart.

It starts with self-observation

Next time you're having a conversation, notice how much time you spend talking. Are you dominating the discussion? After every meeting, take some time to reassess what happened. The reality is, people may forget what you said, but they will never forget how you made them feel. How do your team members feel when you interrupt, talk over them or withhold information? Probably not great. Sure, there are times when you simply need to give instructions without discussion, but those moments should be the exception, not the rule. A great exercise is to use an AI tool to analyse your conversations. It can show you exactly who did most of the talking, and some even measure engagement levels and overall mood. You might be surprised at the results.

The 7-38-55 rule

If you're worried about saying the wrong thing, here's some good news: how you say something is often more important than the words themselves. According to the 7-38-55 rule, popularised by psychologist Albert Mehrabian, communication is broken down to this:

- 7% is verbal (the words you use),
- 38% is vocal (your tone, pitch, speed, intonation), and
- 55% is non-verbal (body language, facial expressions, eye contact).

While the exact percentages can vary by context, your tone and non-verbal cues are more impactful than your actual words. In the workplace, your vocal and non-verbal communication can make the difference between inspiring your team or shutting them down. Think about a meeting situation where you are leaning forward with open body language versus sitting back with crossed arms — it changes the dynamic entirely.

Creating the space for communication

Effective communication is not just about talking and listening — it's also about creating an environment where your team feels safe to speak up. One way to do this is by making space for conversations. Schedule regular one-to-one meetings or ask open-ended questions in team meetings, like 'What else is on your mind?' or 'Any other ideas we haven't considered?' Prompts like these can unlock valuable insights (especially from more introverted members of your team) that you might otherwise miss.

Creating space also means recognising that every time you let your team speak, you might learn something new. Maybe they have the solution to a problem that's been bugging you for weeks. Maybe there's a small issue that's causing unnecessary frustration. Or maybe they've noticed a brewing problem before it's on your radar. Before every interaction, ask yourself: *what can I learn today?*

Preparation matters

To optimise communication, you need to be prepared — at least a little bit. Here are four simple ways to improve your communication:

Smile: Start with a smile and open body language. It sets a positive tone and shows you are ready to listen. And no, I'm not talking about a Cheshire cat creepy smile — just a friendly, relaxed expression will do. Avoid crossing your arms or looking distracted.

Listen: Listening is more than just waiting for your turn to speak. Approach conversations with curiosity and the goal of understanding, not just responding. You will be surprised at how much you learn when you truly listen.

Ask: While listening to the other person, think of questions to ask the speaker based on what they just said. This demonstrates you are listening and shows a genuine interest in what is being said.

Stick to appointments: Whether it's a team meeting or a one-to-one chat, treat internal meetings with the same respect you would an external one. Cancelling or delaying sends the message that your team's concerns are unimportant. If you wouldn't cancel on a client, don't cancel on your team.

Have a plan (at least a little): Before each meeting, think about what you want to achieve. For a team meeting, it could be a clear action plan with specific deadlines. For a one-to-one, it could be checking on work satisfaction or discussing professional development.

Great communication is not just about talking — it's about listening, creating the space and being prepared. When you make better communication a priority, you build trust, get your people engaged and create a team that is motivated to contribute.

Stop doing this:
Ditch these habits for a happier team

As a leader, you are often focused on the big picture, looking to strategise, make plans and grow your business. But sometimes it's the small everyday habits that can quietly undermine all your hard work. From a seemingly harmless after-hours message to assigning the same task to multiple people, these little actions may appear trivial, but to your team they can mean the difference between feeling valued and feeling overlooked, supported or frustrated.

In this section we will shine a light on some of the most common 'leader no-nos'. These habits might not seem like deal-breakers on their own, but collectively they can chip away at trust, morale and productivity. Alongside insights we gained from speaking to employees, I have also included a few universal 'watchouts' from Marshall Goldsmith's bestseller, *What Got You Here Won't Get You There.*

Not giving clear instructions
Picture this: you need something done. You have an idea of how you want it done and you mention it briefly in a meeting. But then days go by and either nothing happens or it gets done differently than you expected. What went wrong? Chances are, your instructions were unclear — maybe you didn't specify who should do it, when it was needed and how to approach the task. If it's not clear who is responsible, everyone assumes someone else will handle it. Without a deadline, there's no urgency and it gets pushed down everybody's to-do lists. If you haven't provided clear guidance, your team may hesitate to ask for clarification, fearing they are bothering you, which ultimately delays progress.

Tip: When assigning a task, nominate one person in charge, set a clear deadline and let them know how to reach you with questions. This ensures accountability, clarity and a timely follow-through.

Tasking two people with the same job
Oh, please don't do this! This usually happens when you've assigned a task to one person (see previous point) but they haven't completed it as quickly as you would like or didn't approach it quite the way you envisioned. So you assign it to someone else — but forget to inform the original person. Suddenly you have two people unknowingly working on the same project. This not only wastes time and resources but can also create tension between even the most understanding employees. It almost always leads to frustration directed at you for the oversight!

Tip: Before reassigning a task, check in with the original person, clarify any misunderstandings and offer guidance if needed to maintain accountability, avoid duplication and keep morale intact.

Not listening
Imagine you are talking to someone, sharing an idea or concern, only to feel that it has barely registered with the other person. That's how your team feels when they are not listened to. Even if your mind is buzzing with a hundred things, being fully present and engaged when your team speaks shows them their insights matter. Interrupting or zoning out may seem harmless, but it quietly sends the message that their ideas and perspectives are not a priority, which discourages future contributions.

Tip: When someone is speaking, focus solely on them. Use active listening techniques, like summarising what they said to show you are fully engaged and value their input.

Failing to recognise and praise
Your team members are putting in effort, often going above and beyond. But if you rarely acknowledge or celebrate their wins, they may feel their work goes unnoticed. Regular recognition is more than just good manners — it builds morale, strengthens loyalty and promotes a culture where people are excited to contribute.

Tip: Make a habit of highlighting individual and team achievements in meetings or quick one-to-one chats. Simple, consistent praise can go a long way towards keeping your team motivated.

Claiming credit that belongs to others
You may not even realise you are doing it, but taking credit for a team member's work, even inadvertently, can create frustration and mistrust. When employees feel their efforts are not acknowledged or are attributed to someone else, it can dampen their enthusiasm and commitment to the team.

Tip: Always give credit where it's due. Publicly recognise the specific contributions of team members to ensure they feel valued and respected for their hard work.

Passing judgement
Constantly judging, even in subtle ways, suppresses openness and creativity. Team members who feel scrutinised for every little detail or feel like their ideas are being ridiculed become cautious, reluctant to take initiative or offer new ideas. Over time, this can lead to a team that sticks to safe choices rather than exploring new ideas and innovation.

Tip: Approach ideas and feedback with curiosity rather than judgement. Encourage a 'no wrong answers' environment to keep the creative energy flowing. Even the most 'out there' idea has at least 10% merit. Try to find the 10%!

Withholding information
In a fast-paced workplace, it's easy to assume some details are not essential to share. However, withholding information, even unintentionally, creates a divide. Without transparency, employees feel out of the loop and less invested, which can lead to misunderstanding and a lack of trust. You also want to avoid the office rumour mill springing into action.

Tip: Communicate openly, even about small developments that may affect the team. A transparent flow of information fosters trust and prevents unnecessary confusion.

Making excuses
Owning up to mistakes can be hard, but nothing erodes credibility faster than passing the blame or making excuses. Your team looks to you as a role model for accountability. If they see you deflecting responsibility, they may feel justified in doing the same, which leads to a culture where mistakes are hidden rather than corrected.

Tip: When things go wrong, accept responsibility and focus on solutions. Modelling accountability builds trust and encourages a proactive, solutions-focused culture.

Missing or postponing an internal meeting
Admit it — you've probably thought, 'Oh, it's only an internal meeting; we can move it,' or maybe you've shown up late to one. Chances are, your team members have done the same. And that's exactly the issue: by treating internal meetings as less important than external ones or other tasks, you're setting a precedent. Remember, your team mirrors your behaviours — if you don't prioritise these internal meetings, they won't either. By arriving late or cancelling, you are subtly sending the message, 'This team is not my priority', which can feel just as dismissive as missing a family dinner.

Tip: Treat internal meetings with the same respect you would give to a VIP client meeting. If a meeting truly is not essential, reconsider whether it needs to happen at all. But once it's in the calendar, honour it — especially one-to-one meetings.

Refusing to apologise
Mistakes happen! But if you're reluctant to apologise, it can come across as arrogant or dismissive. A simple, sincere apology when you've made a mistake shows humility and empathy. Your team will appreciate your willingness to admit mistakes, and it models a healthy approach to handling errors.

Tip: When you slip up, acknowledge it with a genuine apology. This not only maintains trust but also demonstrates that accountability is a value across the team.

Needing to win all the time
There's nothing wrong with ambition but needing to 'win' every interaction or have the final word is exhausting and can make your team feel undervalued and hesitant to share ideas. A collaborative environment needs all voices to be heard and respected without competition getting in the way.

Tip: Practise letting others have the last word in discussions. Showing respect for others' perspectives strengthens your team culture and breeds collaboration.

Requesting meetings without giving a reason

We've all done it: sent a meeting invitation for a future date without including any details — especially if it lands on a Friday for the following week. But this seemingly small oversight can send your team members into a panic loop. The more imaginative (or self-critical) among them may start spiralling, wondering what the meeting could possibly entail. Avoid unnecessary stress by providing at least a bit of context. If it's just a routine check-in, say so. If it's a project update, let them know. If it's a more sensitive discussion, about something like their future with the company, have the courtesy to speak with them directly rather than sending a cold invite.

Tip: Always include a short description of the meeting's purpose in the invitation. It's a simple step that helps your team prepare and keeps their nerves in check.

Messaging outside working hours

Sending messages outside working hours sets a subtle but powerful precedent: 'If I'm thinking about this now, you should be too.' Late-night or weekend messages can send unintended signals, none of which serve you well. It might imply that you're spending your working hours on less-essential tasks and only addressing important topics now, potentially making your team feel that their work — or they themselves — are not a high priority. It also suggests you may struggle to disconnect from work, lack an effective reminder system or, worst of all for team morale, expect them to always be available. I can already hear you protesting: 'I'm just sending emails after hours so I don't forget or because inspiration struck.' In today's always-on world, it is likely your team member will see the notification in real time, disrupting their personal time and sending a subtle message that work doesn't stop.

Tip: Try writing the email as usual but schedule it to send the next workday. This way your team sees it when their workday begins, you don't lose track of your thought and they can enjoy their well-deserved time off.

Hiring the same person over and over again

This might not be something you do consciously, but it happens more often than you would think. Hiring a 'version' of the same person over and over again can result from unconscious bias, comfort with certain personality types or simply relying on gut feeling during interviews. The outcome? A Groundhog Day like repeat of past mistakes and a homogenous team. While possibly harmonious, the new hire may lack variety and the fresh ideas needed to spark innovation.

Tip: The first step is recognising the pattern. Involve diverse voices in the hiring process, actively seeking candidates with different perspectives and skills. This approach not only avoids the repetition trap but also builds a team that is stronger, more dynamic and better prepared for new challenges.

BOSS facts – Part 1

Some truths about leadership are simply non-negotiable. If you've made it this far, you already know that being a great boss isn't just about managing tasks – it's about shaping a culture, making tough calls and leading with intention. But before we move on to structuring, assessing and strategising for your business, let's lay down some undeniable facts about leadership. The following BOSS facts are not just observations; they are truths that will hold up no matter what stage of the journey you're in. Some will challenge your perspective, some will reinforce what you've already learned, but all of them will serve as reminders as you continue building the team and business you truly want. Keep them in mind — they might just be the difference between good intentions and lasting impact.

#1: You absolutely have what it takes, but you can't do it all yourself

Making long-term changes to how things were done up to this point is not an easy feat. It will be tough at times, messy in the middle, and you will possibly want to give up at times. Self-doubt might creep in. The thought that you aren't good enough or don't have what it takes might become your new companion. This psychological phenomenon, called 'Impostor Syndrome', is where someone doubts their own abilities and feels like a fraud or an imposter, despite their qualifications or accomplishments. People with it often believe they are not as competent or intelligent as others and worry they will eventually be found out as a 'fraud'. I am yet to meet a business owner who has not at one point suffered from it, from solopreneurs to multimillion-pound company owners.

With the additional pressure brought on by social media, it's all too easy to feel like you're the only one who has yet to get their life in order. Always remember, looking at someone else's highlight reel means you are comparing your inside to their outside. You don't know anything about their challenges, insecurities or problems. You absolutely have what it takes. You are good enough, and, most importantly, you are worthy of all the success you desire. Of course, there will be moments when you will have to pause, readjust, maybe ask for help and then get going again.

As much as you are ready, you can't (and shouldn't) do it all by yourself. In fact, the bigger and brighter your vision for the future, the more help you'll need to make it happen. Holding on to every task, every decision and every responsibility isn't a sign of dedication — it's a bottleneck and a recipe for burnout. Being a great boss and successful business owner means recognising where your time is best spent and having the courage to let go of the rest. Trust your team. Delegate the things that others can do better and faster. The sooner you step out of the weeds and into true leadership, the stronger your business will be.

#2: Confidence isn't about knowing it all, it's about trusting yourself to figure it out

If you're waiting to feel 100% ready before making a decision or taking action, you'll be waiting forever! Sorry, but someone had to say it. The truth is, confidence doesn't come from having all the answers — it comes from trusting yourself to figure things out as you go. According to Carol Dweck in her book *Mindset*, the most successful people operate with a growth mindset; they believe they can develop new skills and overcome challenges even if they don't have all the information upfront.

You will never have all the answers. Waiting until you are fully ready and know everything there is to know before you start is like planning to drive from London to Edinburgh but only setting off once you can guarantee there won't be any traffic jams, diversions or red lights along the way. You wouldn't do that, would you? You'd rely on your satnav to show you a better alternative route as issues arise on the way. The road will always have bumps and unexpected turns. Don't fall into the 'I'm not ready' trap. The fact that you're thinking about changing something means you are 100% ready. So take the lead, embrace the unknown and trust that you'll figure it out along the way. This is the kind of confidence that not only drives your own success but inspires your team to take on a 'can do' attitude too.

#3: How you do anything is how you do everything

Let's get one thing straight: how you show up in one area of your life reflects how you show up everywhere else. I first came across the phrase 'How you do anything is how you do everything' in T. Harv Eker's *Secrets of the Millionaire Mind*, but it has been echoed by countless personal development leaders like James Clear and Robin Sharma. The message is simple: if you cut corners on the little things, you will cut corners on the big ones too. If you are late to meetings, you're probably late to other commitments in your life. If you let things slide at home, that same slack attitude might show up in your business.

This is not just about doing things right when it *matters* — it's about committing to excellence, even in the smallest of actions. If you avoid looking at your personal finances, you're probably neglecting your business ones too. It is all connected. The truth is, integrity isn't something you turn on and off based on the situation. It needs to be woven into everything you do. Jim Rohn famously said, 'Discipline is the bridge between goals and accomplishment,' and that bridge is built with the small, consistent actions you take every day. These seemingly insignificant choices compound over time, shaping who you are as a leader on the way. So ask yourself: how are you showing up? Are you giving your best effort, even in the mundane moments? Because, ultimately, how you do anything is how you do everything. And if you want your team to be all in, it starts with you being all in — no matter the task.

#4: Keep it FAB

Sometimes you will need to have difficult conversations with your team — whether in a group session or a one-to-one meeting. It's perfectly normal to feel a bit nervous about these situations. After all, nobody likes to be the bearer of bad news or potentially upset someone. To help you stay focused during the meeting and avoid getting too personal or sidetracked, try using the FAB framework.

Focus: Before going into the meeting, be clear about the issue. What is the one thing you need to address? If you need to tell a member of your team to stop doing something or critique their work, focus on the behaviour, not their character. In a team meeting, stay laser focused on the desired outcome (e.g. finalising the details of a new marketing campaign). Focusing your energy helps you cut through the noise, keeps the conversation on track and prevents overwhelm and confusion.

Action: Once you've addressed the issue or topic, agree on the specific actions you or your team will take. This shifts the focus forward, rather than dwelling on why something went wrong. For a one-to-one conversation, define the specific behaviours you want to see improved or outline the support you will provide to help them succeed. In a team setting, clearly define which actions need to be completed before the next meeting and by whom. Being specific ensures productivity and demonstrates you are future-focused and ready to get things done.

Breathe: After the meeting, take a moment to breathe and assess how it went. Did you achieve the outcome you intended? If not, reflect on what you can improve next time. But don't just focus on what could have been better — also take note of what went well. Recognising successes, no matter how small, helps reinforce good habits and builds confidence. Regularly reflecting on both wins and lessons learned will make you a more reflective and productive leader in the long run.

By keeping it FAB, you can navigate challenges with confidence and turn what feels like chaos into manageable steps. Let it be your go-to strategy when you're feeling nervous, anxious or overwhelmed — so you can keep moving forward, no matter what comes your way.

2. Organise the Ideal

In this chapter, we build the framework for an ideal business structure — the foundation that will bring your vision to life. Each part of this chapter will walk you through critical steps to clarify the direction, define roles and streamline processes. As Michael E. Gerber explains in *The E-Myth Revisited*, too many business owners get bogged down by day-to-day firefighting without a clear idea where they are going. The result? They work *in* their business rather than *on* it, meaning tasks that benefit the growth and direction are first to fall off the to-do list. By stepping back and thinking strategically about where you want to go, you lay the groundwork for a business that can grow sustainably and run independently.

First, we will focus on the importance of dreaming big and setting clear, meaningful goals. Before you build a team structure or streamline workflows, it is crucial to know your destination. This clarity will guide every decision you make and will ensure each part of your business machine is moving in harmony with your vision.

Second, we will take a close look at how you are currently spending your time, what tasks you are involved in, where your energy goes and how your role fits into the bigger picture. This will be the foundation for designing your ideal day and ensuring your focus is on the work that truly moves the business forward. From there, we'll start shaping your ideal organisational structure, creating role clarity and defining responsibilities that allow both you and your team to operate at your best.

Where are you going?

If you take away only one thing from this book, let it be the exercises in this chapter. It might sound bold, but if you approach it with focus, time and seriousness, this chapter has the potential to change the direction of your business and your life. Too many business owners wake up each day and dive straight into the demands of the moment, only focusing on the week ahead or the next holiday or weekend. Over time, we become passive bystanders in our own lives, forgetting that we actually have the power to choose our direction.

We are not defined by what happens to us, but rather by how we respond. We are response-ABLE — we can choose how we respond to any situation. To respond in a way that suits our long-term plan, we need to have one. In order to respond with intention, we need a clear destination. As Stephen Covey explains in *The 7 Habits of Highly Effective People*, beginning with the end in mind is essential. Without a compelling vision, it is too easy to get lost in the day-to-day distractions. With a clear purpose, each decision becomes a step towards our larger goals.

So, what's driving you? If your mind hesitates or you can't immediately answer, remember this: businesses built with a strong, purpose-driven vision tend to endure longer and are more resilient when faced with challenges. By 'purpose-driven', I don't mean solely profit-focused or growth-obsessed. A purpose-driven business is one motivated by a mission bigger than just one person — a vision of leaving a positive mark on the world. A larger purpose will motivate you when the going gets tough and will lift you up when you need it.

Take Patagonia, for example, a company built on a purpose much larger than profit alone. The company is driven by a mission to protect and preserve the environment. Patagonia has weathered numerous challenges, from economic downturns to public backlash against the fashion industry's environmental impact. Instead of compromising, they doubled down on their mission and even urged their customers to 'buy less' and promoted repair over replacement.

Their strong commitment to their purpose has not only created millions of loyal advocating fans around the world but also strengthened their resolve through every challenge. This is what happens when a business is driven by a larger purpose: it becomes more resilient, attracts more people who believe in its mission and sustains itself in difficult times. Your purpose doesn't have to be monumental, like solving world hunger. It can be making a positive difference in your area, building a positive workplace, or providing a product or service that genuinely improves lives. The key is that it is meaningful to you.

In the following exercises, we will do two things:

1. **Create your vision and decide what you want**
   As the business owner, your happiness and wellbeing directly impact your team. When you feel fulfilled and energised, it cascades through the entire business. Together, we will clarify what you truly want in life and business. We will explore your long-term goals for the company to build a vision that will guide not only you but your team as well.

2. **Strengthen your commitment to these goals**
   To make these goals even more solid and almost real enough to touch, we will use powerful exercises like visualisation, journalling and vision boards. These techniques help reinforce your vision by activating your subconscious to recognise opportunities and stay focused on achieving your goals. By regularly connecting with your goals, you are more likely to make choices that align with your vision.

For these exercises, let go of overthinking and self-doubt. Just run with whatever comes to mind — there is no right or wrong here. It's your business; you get to make the rules. If you decide your office needs a slide instead of stairs, a mandatory Friday afternoon dance party or a full-sized pirate ship on the roof for 'team-building exercises', so be it. The right people will stay with you and be completely on board with whatever you decide (probably hoisting the Jolly Roger before you even ask). In fact, they might take your idea and make it even better — turning that pirate ship into a floating meeting room or the ultimate Friday happy hour spot. Give yourself permission to dream big, have fun and trust that the best ideas often come from thinking outside the box.

Don't be limited by the 'how' — we'll get to that later. For now, simply dream big and be honest with yourself about what you truly desire. As with all exercises, give yourself the time specified (as a minimum) without interruptions and go somewhere that puts you in a positive mood. If your house frustrates you because you never got around to painting the walls or you need to fix a thousand things, don't do it at home. Go to a happy place. Pick a coffee shop, coworking space or whatever locality provides the right setting.

While I encourage you to dedicate at least half an hour to each exercise initially, don't rush to complete them all in one sitting. These are big, important questions that deserve time to unfold. Let the ideas and questions linger in your mind over the next few days. Pay attention to the things in your current life or business that no longer serve you, the frustrations you have accepted as 'normal' and the moments (and people) that genuinely light you up. Sometimes clarity comes not from forcing answers but from observing your reactions and allowing space for inspiration to strike. Think of this process as planting seeds — nurture them with time and reflection and they will grow into a vision you feel truly excited to pursue.

Exercise: Envision your ideal life
30 minutes

Let's start by envisioning your ideal life. What does a 'happy life' look like to you? Consider questions like:

- Where do you live?
- How often do you travel and who is with you?
- How much money do you need?
- How do you spend your spare time?
- How many days a week do you work?
- What are your non-negotiables in life? (e.g. time with family, creative outlets, health routines, etc.)
- What brings you the most fulfilment and how does your ideal life incorporate more of it?
- When was the last time you felt truly satisfied and content? What were you doing then?
- Who do you envision spending time with? What qualities do they bring into your life?

_____

_____

_____

_____

_____

_____

_____

_____

Based on your answers to those questions, you can now work out how much money you will need to enable your ideal lifestyle.

And before my 'creative visionaries' and 'big-picture thinkers' start panicking — yes, I mean you, the one who sees a spreadsheet and suddenly remembers they have literally anything else to do. This is not a maths test. No one is asking for a perfectly balanced budget. Rough estimates are completely fine. The goal is clarity, not accounting perfection — so don't use maths (arrrgh!) as an excuse to skip this part.

On the flip side, if you're the type who loves accuracy, you might already feel the creeping urge to *adjust* your vision now that real numbers are involved. Suddenly, that dream beach house feels a little too extravagant, the luxury holidays become long weekends in Cornwall and you are rationalising why you probably don't need a personal chef after all. Stop right there! This exercise isn't about what feels realistic *right now* — it is about defining what you actually want. Don't shrink your vision before you've even started working towards it.

Start by listing the key elements of your vision: the home you want to live in, the holidays you want to take, the quality of life you want to provide for your family, the personal investments you want to make (such as education or hobbies) and the level of financial security you want through savings or investments.

Add up the approximate costs for these elements to calculate the annual income you would need to sustain this lifestyle. For example, imagine your vision includes living in a spacious family home (£3,000 per month), taking three memorable family holidays a year (£12,000 each) and setting aside £1,000 a month for savings and investments. In this case, your ideal personal annual income target might be £87,000.

Once you've established this figure, ask yourself: what does my business need to generate in profit to make this possible? This is the first tangible benchmark for your business to aim at. Knowing this number will give you clarity and purpose — it's no longer just about growing the business for the sake of growth but about creating the life you envisioned. Keep in mind this target may evolve as your goals or circumstances change, but having this initial benchmark will give you a clear starting point.

Envision your ideal business
30 minutes

Now you've created a monetary target for your ideal lifestyle, it's time to envision the business that will make that lifestyle possible. What does your business look like when it's 'finished'? Keep in mind that 'finished' will mean different things to different people — it could mean selling the business, creating a lasting legacy or simply reaching a point where your business runs so smoothly and independently that you feel you've 'made it'. Take a moment to reflect on this vision and let yourself dream big. Use the following questions to shape your ideas:

- What is the annual profit goal (remember, focus on *profit*, not turnover)?
- How big is your team? What is your business's geographical reach?
- What legacy do you want your business to leave, both in the industry and in the lives of others?
- If you could remove one current frustration from your business life, what would it be?
- What core values do you want your business to embody? How would these values show in day-to-day operations? (We'll work on values in more detail later, but it's a good idea to start thinking about them here.)

_____

_____

_____

_____

_____

_____

_____

As you work through these questions, visualise the details of your 'finished' business. Picture the systems, the structure and the feeling of success that aligns with your definition of a fulfilling business.

Envision your ideal team
30 minutes

Once you've envisioned your ideal business, the next step is to reflect on the people who will help bring that vision to life. A business is only as strong as the team behind it, so it's essential to set your intention for the kind of team you want to build. Even though you can't control every aspect of how your team operates, creating a clear picture of your ideal team will help you subconsciously attract the right people and provide an environment where they can flourish. By envisioning your ideal team, you are not only shaping the culture and dynamics of your workplace but also paving the way for the kind of collaboration, innovation and problem-solving that will help you achieve your wider business goals.

To get started, ask yourself the following questions:

- If you could describe the perfect team culture in three words, what are they and why?
- How does your team handle challenges and setbacks? What qualities do they demonstrate in those moments?
- What qualities do you want each team member to embody, beyond skills or qualifications?
- How does your team communicate and collaborate with each other?

_____

_____

_____

_____

_____

_____

Take your time with these questions and let yourself imagine your team in action. What does it feel like to walk into the office or join a team meeting? How do your team members support one another? How do they represent your business to customers or clients? By creating a clear picture of your ideal team, you are setting the foundation for a strong, aligned and motivated group of individuals who will help make your vision a reality.

What are you doing?

It is all too easy to get caught up in the day-to-day grind, doing things the way they've always been done, reacting instead of initiating and filling your days with tasks that keep you busy but aren't actually moving you forward or making you feel fulfilled. Without realising it, you might be spending precious time on things that drain your energy, slow your progress or could easily be handled by someone else.

Now that you have a clearer vision of where you're heading, it's time to take a hard look at how you're actually spending your time. This chapter isn't about what you *should* be doing — it's about reclaiming your time and making sure your role in the business aligns with your strengths, natural talents and long-term goals. For this exercise, we'll break down the tasks that currently fill your days and evaluate which ones you want to keep, delegate or ditch entirely. The goal is to build a setup that works *for* you, not one that keeps you stuck on autopilot.

Exercise: Conduct a task audit
30 minutes

Find a quiet place where you can work without interruptions. Take some time and list all the tasks you're currently involved in, all the processes you oversee and all the decisions that are being run past you. Include everything, from the essential tasks that only you, as the business owner, can do to all those you're still doing because you don't trust anyone else to take them on or you haven't found the right person with the necessary skills. Don't overthink — just write them down.

To get the most accurate picture, I highly recommend tracking your tasks over the course of a week or two rather than trying to list them all in one go. You'll be surprised at how much time actually goes into certain activities versus what you *think* you spend on them. To make this easier, you'll find a simple tracking template on www.takecharge-thebook.com — use it to jot down everything that occupies your time throughout the day. This approach gives you a far more realistic view than making a list in isolation, away from the actual hustle of your workday.

As you track your tasks, also consider how much time you spend on each of them and how often you find yourself procrastinating because they don't come naturally to you or drain your energy.

To make a start on your list, here are a few key areas to consider:

Lead generation
- Developing strategies to attract new clients.
- Networking and attending events.
- Creating and managing partnerships or referral programmes.

Sales
- Conducting sales calls or meetings.
- Creating proposals and closing deals.
- Following up with potential clients or leads.
- Managing CRM systems and sales pipelines.

Marketing
- Creating content for social media, blogs or newsletters.
- Managing advertising campaigns.
- Designing promotional materials.
- Planning and executing marketing strategies.

Customer service
- Responding to customer enquiries.
- Handling complaints or resolving issues.
- Gathering customer feedback and reviews.
- Managing customer loyalty programmes.

Production
- Overseeing product development from concept to completion.
- Managing supply chains and inventory.
- Quality control and testing.
- Coordinating with suppliers.

Delivery
- Ensuring timely and accurate delivery of products and services.
- Managing logistics and distribution channels.
- Handling shipping, returns or exchanges.

Aftercare
- Following up with customers after a purchase.
- Offering support and troubleshooting.
- Providing ongoing training or resources to clients.

Human resources
- Conducting performance reviews and feedback sessions.
- Training and developing your team.
- Recruiting, interviewing and onboarding new hires.

IT and technology
- Overseeing website maintenance and updates.
- Managing software, tools and systems.
- Troubleshooting tech issues.
- Ensuring cybersecurity and data protection.

Finance and accounting
- Reviewing financial reports.
- Managing budgets, cash flow and forecasting.
- Handling tax filings and compliance.

Day-to-day operations
- Scheduling and managing calendars.
- Ordering office supplies and managing inventory.
- Organising meetings and team events.

Office management
- Keeping the office clean and organised.
- Handling maintenance tasks (e.g. cleaning the coffee machine).
- Ensuring utilities and supplies (like toilet paper) are stocked.

Once you have your list, take a step back and look at what takes up your time. What stands out? Were there any surprises? Did you realise you're spending far more time on certain tasks than you thought? Or maybe you've spotted things you probably shouldn't be doing but have been holding on to out of habit? This exercise isn't just about writing down what you do — it is about gaining awareness where your time and energy actually go.

Before we move on, take a moment to reflect:

- which tasks drain you the most?
- which ones excite you and play to your strengths?
- are there tasks you've been holding on to that someone else could handle just as well — or better?

Now that you have assessed where your time is going, it's time to shift focus to the tasks that truly belong to you as the business owner. Many business owners I speak to would rather avoid these responsibilities, but if you want to be the best boss your business could possibly have, you'll need to put on your 'big boss pants' and take ownership.

It's easy to get stuck doing things you should have delegated long ago while avoiding the things that actually require your leadership. As your business grows, your role needs to evolve too. If you haven't fully stepped into these responsibilities yet, now's the time to *take charge*. And don't worry, we'll take a deeper dive into which tasks to keep, delegate or ditch in the next exercise. But for now, let's look at the tasks where you need to step up:

Strategic planning and vision setting. You are the one setting the direction (hence we spent so much time on it previously). No one else in your business should be deciding the long-term vision or strategy. If you're still too involved in day-to-day business to make time for this, it's time to step back and set out your destination clearly.

Company culture and values. Whether you've defined it or not, your company already has a culture — the one you tolerate. As the business owner, it's your responsibility to set and nurture a culture that aligns with your goals for productivity, profitability and staff fulfilment. While your team can (and should) contribute to shaping it, the final say has to come from you. Culture isn't just about words on a wall, it's built through the behaviours you encourage, the values you uphold and the actions you take (or don't take) as a leader.

We'll dive deeper into *how* to establish and reinforce the right culture in Chapter 4, but for now, recognise that this is one of the most critical areas where you need to show up.

Critical decision making. Some decisions are too important to delegate — not because your team isn't capable, but because they require your strategic vision and leadership. Major investments, strategic pivots and hiring key team members don't just impact the business today but define its future. You can gather advice, involve your team and weigh the data, but at the end of the day, these are the calls only you can make.

Financial oversight. You can (and probably should) delegate bookkeeping and accounting tasks, but understanding your numbers is non-negotiable. Every business owner needs to be able to look at and interpret their profit and loss statement: if you don't know where your money is coming from, where it's going and what that means for your business, you are flying blind. Financial oversight includes regularly reviewing reports, managing cash flow and making high-level financial decisions. You don't need to be an accountant, but you do need to know enough to make informed choices and spot potential issues before they become serious problems.

Brand identity and reputation management. Your brand is your reputation, and while you don't need to manage every detail of marketing or PR, you do need to protect its integrity. Your role isn't to execute marketing tasks — it's to ensure your brand remains aligned with your vision and values. Hire professionals to handle the execution of branding, messaging and public relations, but stay involved enough to maintain consistency. If the way your business is presented to the world starts to feel 'off', it is up to you to course-correct. Think of yourself as the guardian of your brand's essence — you set the standard, and it's your job to ensure everything reflects what your business truly stands for.

Crisis management. A crisis is when your leadership is needed more than ever. In tough times — whether financial challenges, operational setbacks or a PR disaster — your team will look to you for direction. This isn't the time to disappear into strategy meetings or panic behind closed doors. You need to be seen taking charge, setting the course and filling your team with the vision and confidence they need to do their job. That doesn't mean micromanaging every response, but it does mean providing clear direction that reflects your company's vision and values. Your role in a crisis is not to solve every problem yourself but to steer the ship: offering clarity, making key decisions and ensuring your team stays united in turbulent waters.

> ## Exercise: Defining your ideal role
> 30 minutes
>
> Now that you have a clearer picture of where your time is going, it's time to make some decisions. The goal is to eliminate, delegate or optimise anything that doesn't belong on your plate so that your time is spent on the tasks that truly move your business forward. For this, we will use the concept of your 'Zone of Genius', which was first introduced by Gay Hendricks in *The Big Leap*. The four zones you can operate in are:
>
> ### The Zone of Incompetence
>
> These are tasks you are simply not good at and that drain your energy. You may currently be handling these out of necessity, but they are not where you should be focusing your time.
>
> ### The Zone of Competence
>
> Here you are doing tasks that you are reasonably good at but you are no better at than most other people. These might include things you had to learn over time, like bookkeeping or basic IT troubleshooting. While you can do these things, they don't bring you fulfilment, and someone else could handle them just as effectively (if not better).

The Zone of Excellence

In this zone, you are actually quite good at what you're doing. You've practised the skills and have become highly proficient. These might even be tasks people come to you for, but they don't necessarily ignite your passion. They can be a comfort zone but will probably not lead to any personal or professional growth.

The Zone of Genius

Here your natural talents, passions and unique abilities come together, where you find yourself in a state of 'flow' — you get fully immersed, are highly productive and feel deeply satisfied. These are the activities that feel almost effortless to you and make a significant impact on your business.

How to use this framework

Step 1: Go through the task list you created earlier and highlight the activities that fall into your Zone of Genius — those tasks that energise you, come naturally and make the most significant impact. These are the ones you want to prioritise in your ideal business setup. Mark these with a colour.

Step 2: Now go through the list again and mark all the tasks that fall into your Zone of Competence or Zone of Incompetence with a different colour. These are all the things that drain your energy, slow you down or could be done just as well (or better) by someone else.

You have just marked all the tasks to delegate or outsource: before assigning a task to someone else, ask yourself if technology could eliminate it altogether. The goal isn't to move tasks from one to-do list to another but to streamline your business as much as possible. For the tasks that can't be automated or eliminated, identify who in your team could take them on. If no one is currently responsible or suitable, consider training, hiring for the role or outsourcing.

Step 3: The hardest category to deal with is the Zone of Excellence. These are the tasks you're really good at but don't necessarily enjoy or need to be doing. The problem? They often take up a lot of time, and because you are great at them, you convince yourself you *should* keep them. But be honest: do these tasks really light you up? Or are you holding on to them out of habit, necessity or fear no one else will do them as well as you? If they don't align with your long-term vision or take time away from higher-impact work, it is time to delegate or outsource them. That doesn't mean you have to let go of everything. If there are tasks you genuinely love (and they are not just keeping you in your comfort zone), by all means, keep them. But if you're clinging to certain responsibilities simply because you don't trust anyone else with them, recognise that at some point, you'll have to let go if you want to grow the business. Your time and energy are limited, and the more you hold on to tasks that someone else could handle, the less capacity you have for the things only you should be doing.

Step 4: Make a separate list with only the tasks from your Zone of Genius and the non-negotiable business owner tasks we discussed earlier. This is your new to-do list — the tasks that come first, no discussion. Time must be scheduled for them and they are to be completed before anything else. You can still spend your time on other activities, but these are priority one. Everything else comes second (or even third). In the following chapters, we will look at strategies to ensure all remaining tasks are taken care of to free you up to focus on what really matters.

How are you doing it?

It's hierarchy time! Yes, this is the bit where you get to create your ideal organisational structure. You are building your very own empire. What does your company look like? You are at the top as the owner, but what does the rest of the structure look like? Are you still running the day-to-day operations or do you have a manager doing that for you? Do you want to handle all tasks in-house or are there some areas that can be outsourced?

The topic of hierarchy is probably one of the most debated in the business world. Many companies swear by a more lenient, flexible approach when it comes to structuring their teams. They believe rigid hierarchies are only for big corporate businesses. And the truth is, a laissez-faire style can work for some businesses — emphasis on can and some — IF you have the right people on your team, they know exactly what they are doing, understand who handles tasks when someone is away and maintain accountability. If everyone knows their responsibilities and no task is duplicated or neglected, you might not need a formal structure. However (and it is a big *however*), chances are, things don't always run that smoothly in your organisation. Maybe there are frequent misunderstandings about who is responsible for what, or maybe your team feels overwhelmed or disengaged because expectations are unclear.

So, does your business need a hierarchy? This depends on several factors: the size of the team, the nature of your work, your business goals and the dynamics within your team. As your business grows, coordination and communication naturally become more complex, and defining clear roles prevents confusion and inefficiencies. For businesses that prioritise creativity and innovation, a flatter structure might work better because it encourages communication, collaboration and the free flow of ideas. In contrast, process-driven businesses often benefit from a hierarchy that ensures consistency, quality control and efficient decision-making.

Even the smallest business needs to consider scalability. As your team grows, your hierarchy will naturally evolve. While smaller teams often function best with a simple, functional structure, businesses with larger teams or more diverse offerings may eventually explore more complex options, such as product-based hierarchies. For now, focus on building a structure that provides clear roles, responsibilities and accountability at your current size. The key is scalability — creating a foundation that can grow with you as your business expands.

We are not trying to build a rigid structure that doubles the time it takes to get things done because of all the red tape. What we want is a flexible structure that provides clarity, improves efficiency and supports the future growth of the business. The key is to find the balance that aligns with your goals (both personal and business), the nature of your work and your operational needs. We are after a sense of structure — enough to provide clear responsibilities and reporting duties but not so rigid, it turns the office into a soulless enterprise where everyone says, 'That's not my job.' The goal is to strike a balance: enough structure to clarify who is responsible for what without stifling flexibility and innovation.

In an informal LinkedIn poll I conducted, over 60% of participants agreed that having some structure while remaining adaptable is the ideal way forward. 32% of participants leaned towards a more rigid hierarchy, and the rest did not believe in any form of structure. While not a scientific study, this feedback reflects what many business owners and employees intuitively know: balance is key. Research supports this perspective: a study by Effectory found that 86% of employees with high role clarity report high levels of effectiveness, while 84% of them expressed the intention to stay and 75% also reported high levels of leadership satisfaction. The same study showed that employees who experience role clarity are 53% more efficient and 27% more effective than those operating in ambiguity.[13]

'What's the difference between efficiency and effectiveness?' I hear you ask. Let's say your business has a team member tasked with sending invoices. If they are efficient, they will send out all the invoices quickly and without time wasted — great for productivity. But if they are also effective, they will send the invoices to the right clients, with the correct amounts and terms, ensuring the desired outcome. Clarity in roles ensures not just speed but also accuracy, which ultimately drives better results. From my own experience, having worked in companies with flat structures, rigid hierarchies and no structure whatsoever, I can confirm that structure alone is not the silver bullet for a great business. But it *can* serve as an important pillar to build from — with the right balance, structure can provide a foundation for growth, innovation and employee satisfaction.

Exercise: The structure-maker
30—60 minutes

Part 1

This is your chance to create the ideal structure for your business. Based on the tasks you identified that you no longer want to handle, think about the kind of support you need to offload those responsibilities. What roles do you need to allow you to focus on your Zone of Genius? What tasks would each of these roles take on?

Step 1: Reflect on the goals you set in Chapter 1 and ask yourself what kind of organisational structure is required to make those dreams a reality. If, for example, you don't want to be interrupted constantly, you might need a senior management level that acts as a filter so only critical issues get to you. Or if you want to only work one day a week, you may need a managing director to run operations during the other four days who only consults you on major decisions.

Step 2: Create an organisational chart that makes sense for your ideal future. Don't think about the people currently on your team. Imagine you are starting from scratch. What would the structure look like if you were designing it today? Don't tie it to what exists now — you are the boss and you get to design your business the way you want.

Part 2

Now that you've created the structure, assign the tasks you identified in the previous exercise to these roles. We'll be making a detailed list of all the tasks that keep the business running in Chapter 3, but for now, focus on assigning the tasks you no longer want or need to do. If it's easier, start by assigning tasks to departments rather than individual roles. Once each department has its responsibilities, you can break those tasks into specific roles.

Part 3

Stress-test time! Now you have designed your ideal organisational structure, ask yourself these questions:

- Does the structure support your long-term business goals?
- Does the structure support your personal goals?
- Does every key function (sales, marketing, operations, finance, etc.) have a clear place?
- Does each department clearly contribute to the overall objectives?
- Are communication and reporting lines clear? Is decision-making authority evenly distributed?
- Can this structure handle hypothetical scenarios like launching a new product or managing a crisis?

> If you answered 'yes' to all these questions, congratulations! You've just created a blueprint for your company's future. Even if the chart includes more roles than you currently have people for, you have set a clear destination. Use it as a guide for hiring, firing and restructuring decisions as you grow.

Once you've defined your ideal organisational structure, it's time to get even more specific about how you want your business to run on a day-to-day basis. A well-structured team is important, but clarity in expectations, decision-making and boundaries is what keeps everything running smoothly. Now it's time to establish how you want your business to run, how decisions are made and what you, as the boss, will and won't tolerate.

Setting the boss rules: Creating boundaries and expectations

One of the best things about being the boss? You get to set the rules.

These are your non-negotiables, the way you want things to be done, no explanations required. Later, we'll define the rules for your team, but for now, this is about you: how you work, how decisions are made and what you will and won't tolerate. This is your business and these are the rules of the game.

Of course, that doesn't mean going overboard with wild 'diva-like' demands. Asking your team to perform a little dance before entering your office probably won't make you very popular. These rules should make your life easier, not create unnecessary friction. Below are some key areas to consider for defining your boss rules and setting the foundation for a business that works on your terms.

Accessibility and communication.

These rules clarify how you want to be approached by your team and how communication should flow within the organisation.

Examples:
- No work-related emails or messages after 6 p.m. unless it's an emergency.
- Regular updates to be sent via email, with phone calls reserved for urgent issues.
- Weekly 30-minute check-ins with direct reports during set office hours.

Questions to consider:
- How available do you want to be to your team? Is an open-door policy your style, or would you prefer set hours for one-on-one discussions?
- Should team members message you first or is it acceptable to come and see you for a quick chat?
- How quickly do you want your team to respond to emails or messages? Do response times vary by urgency?

Legal and compliance.

These rules ensure your business stays compliant with industry regulations and protects sensitive information.

Examples:
- All client information must be stored securely and accessed only by authorised personnel.
- Compliance training sessions are mandatory for all new hires.
- Non-disclosure agreements must be signed before working with external contractors.

Questions to consider:
- What protocols do you need to put in place to protect client data and confidentiality?

- How will you ensure compliance with industry regulations? What training is necessary for your team?
- How should your team handle sensitive information to prevent data breaches?

Decision-making and autonomy.
These rules set the boundaries for how much authority your team has and when they need to involve you in decisions.

Examples:
- Team leads can approve expenses up to £500 without additional approval.
- Client proposals over £5,000 require a review and sign-off from you.
- Department heads can decide on new hires for their teams but must consult you for senior roles.

Questions to consider:
- What decisions can your team make on their own? How much risk are you comfortable with them taking?
- Are certain people granted budgetary authority? If so, up to what amount?
- Are there topics where your team has full decision-making freedom?

Respecting boundaries and work–life balance.
These rules ensure your team maintains a healthy balance between work and personal life while also respecting each other's time.

Examples:
- No meetings before 9 a.m. or after 4 p.m. to allow for uninterrupted work time.
- Holiday requests must be submitted at least two weeks in advance, except in emergencies.
- Team members are encouraged to log off completely during weekends and holidays.

Questions to consider:
- How will you ensure your team respects personal boundaries, like not working after hours or during weekends?
- What are your guidelines for taking time off or handling unexpected absences?
- How can you demonstrate your commitment to your team's work—life balance?

Accountability and core values in action.
These rules set expectations for accountability, ensuring the team aligns with the company's values in every action.

Examples:
- Clear deadlines must be met and any delays communicated at least 48 hours in advance.
- Honesty and transparency are expected in all team communications.
- Any breach of confidentiality will result in immediate disciplinary action.

Questions to consider:
- How will you ensure your team stays accountable to deadlines and commitments?
- How do you want to encourage honesty and transparency within your team?
- What actions will you take if someone fails to uphold your core values?

Confidentiality and privacy.
These rules are essential for protecting your clients, your team and your business.

Examples:
- No discussing client projects in public spaces or online forums.
- All employees must sign a confidentiality agreement upon hiring.
- Only authorised personnel can access sensitive data.

Questions to consider:
- How will you protect client and company data from breaches?
- What measures will you put in place to ensure confidentiality is maintained?
- How will you enforce these rules if they're breached?

Feedback, appraisals and continuous improvement.
These rules help ensure performance is regularly reviewed and feedback is given constructively.

Examples:
- Monthly one-on-one meetings with direct reports to review progress and provide feedback.
- Constructive feedback should be given privately, not in front of the team.
- Annual performance appraisals to discuss career growth and development.

Questions to consider:
- How often do you want to conduct performance reviews? What's the preferred format (formal meetings, quick check-ins)?
- How should feedback be delivered — both positive and constructive?
- How will you support continuous improvement in your team's performance?

Work location and flexibility.
These rules set expectations around where and how your team can work to accommodate different needs and preferences.

Examples:
- Team members can work remotely up to three days per week, with Mondays and Wednesdays reserved as in-office collaboration days.
- All employees must be available online between the core hours of 10 a.m. and 3 p.m., regardless of their location.

- Hybrid working is encouraged, but key meetings (quarterly reviews, strategy sessions) must be attended in person unless approved otherwise.

Questions to consider:
- Where do you expect your team to work from? Are you okay with remote work or do you prefer everyone to be in the office?
- Is hybrid working an option? If so, what are the parameters (e.g. specific days in the office)?
- Can team members work from abroad if needed? What guidelines should they follow if working remotely from a different country?
- Do you want to establish core hours when everyone must be online and available?

Grab your notebook and jot down your answers to the questions above. Be as specific as possible. Add anything else that comes to mind. These non-negotiables will form the backbone of your management style and will guide how your team operates. Once you've defined what you are not willing to compromise on, let's dive into an exercise to visualise your perfect day. This will help you bring your rules and your ideal organisational structure to life by imagining how it will all fit into your daily routine.

Exercise: Design your perfect day
30 minutes

Imagine it is five years from now and your business is running exactly how you have always dreamed. Start from the moment you wake up.
- What does your morning routine look like?
- How do you start your workday? What tasks or meetings do you have?

As you walk through your day, pay attention to how your team functions.
- Who handles client enquiries?
- Who manages operations and keeps everything running smoothly?
- What decisions are brought to you? Which ones are handled by others?

Write out your ideal day in detail. Focus on what your role is, how your team supports you and how the structure you have created plays out in real life.

This exercise not only helps you visualise your ideal structure but also gives you a clearer picture of what you need to focus on to bring this vision to life.

How to make it stick

Setting a big colourful vision for yourself and your business can feel daunting, especially if this kind of reflective work is new to you. Below, you will find three different techniques to help you bring your vision to life. Each one is slightly different in the way it makes your dreams more 'real'. I encourage you to try each one, but remember, you don't need to do them all — simply try them and then continue with the one that resonates with you the most. Let them be tools you can come back to whenever you need a boost in clarity or motivation.

Vision board

A vision board is a visual representation of your dreams and goals. It helps you 'see' your future as a daily reminder of what you are working towards. It's your permission to go wild. It lets you tap into your creative side by pulling together images, words and symbols that align with your vision. This is a great exercise in which to involve your spouse and family. It sparks conversations and is a great way to get your friends and family on board with your goals.

Gather materials. Grab a board or a large sheet of paper, scissors, glue, magazines or printouts of images that inspire you — things you want to do, places you want to see, people you want to spend more time with, etc. You can also create a digital version using a platform like Pinterest.

Using your answers from the previous exercises, go through the magazines and images and pick anything that aligns with your vision. Look for visuals that bring up positive emotions and represent aspects of your ideal life and business.

Arrange your images and words on your board to create a collage that captures your goals. Place the board somewhere you will see it often, like your office or home.

The future self

This exercise invites you to picture a day in the life of your ideal future self and to imagine what your life and business will look like once you've achieved your goals. It taps into your imagination and will help you feel more connected to your vision on an emotional level.

Find a quiet, comfortable space and close your eyes.

Imagine yourself five or ten years from now, living your ideal life. Walk through a day in your future self's shoes. Where are you? What are you doing in the morning, afternoon, evening?

Pay attention to detail. What does your workspace look like? Who is around you? How do you feel as you go through the day?

After visualising (give yourself at least ten minutes. Set a timer if you're worried about losing track of time or falling asleep), write down what you have experienced. Describe it as if you're actually telling someone about your day. This will be your reminder of the life you're working towards. Read it every day.

Journalling

Journalling is a great way to reflect on your goals regularly. It helps you stay connected to your vision and allows you to make adjustments over time. This exercise can be as structured or as freestyle as you like and allows you to tune in to your goals and the actions needed to achieve them.

Dedicate a special notebook for this exercise and set time aside every day or week to write.

Reflect on successes and setbacks. Ask yourself what's working well, what challenges you're facing and any adjustments you might deem necessary. Alternatively, you can begin each writing session with a prompt like 'What is one step I can take today that moves me closer to my vision?' or 'What excites me about my vision right now?'

Allow your journal to be a personal dialogue. There are no rules — start writing and sees where it takes you. I'd suggest giving yourself a minimum amount of time to write for, especially on days when you don't feel like it. The best results usually come after the initial thoughts, when you think you don't have anything more to write.

Congratulations! By completing this chapter, you have created your individual blueprint for an organised, efficient company that is aligned with your goals. In Chapter 3 we move from theory to practice — we will be looking at your current team and structure to start making your vision a reality.

BOSS facts – Part 2

#5: Your team is not your family

Yup, there you go. I said it. Your colleagues and team at work are not your family. Instead, what you are aiming for is a team like a successful sports team. In a sports team, every player has a specific role and understands exactly how their position contributes to the overall goal. Teams and players are evaluated based on measurable outcomes. They are always training, always improving, investing the time and money to get better. There are set standards everyone is held to — each player has a responsibility for the team's success or failure. In sports, successes are celebrated, whether they are small wins or big milestones.

For a team to be truly great, its members need to trust each other. They might not be best friends, but once they step onto the pitch, field or court, they know they can count on each other. That said, many teammates do form strong bonds. They share many highs and lows, and it's only natural that friendships develop over time. Team members look out for one another; they listen, they support and they see how they can help. There are countless examples of professional athletes struggling with injuries, anxiety, depression and other emotional or physical challenges only to have their teammates rally around them to defend them both publicly and privately. Just like any professional sports team, your team will need a great coach (= leader and manager) — someone who is not just focused on performance but on the wellbeing of the individual players too. It's the coach's job to ensure that team members aren't just working hard but are also getting the support they need. This means checking in with your people, making sure they are heard and ensuring they have access to resources (whether medical, psychological or personal development) that allow them to show up at their best.

Team members also have fun doing what they do — they joined their sport because they are passionate about it and they stay because of that love. Great teams must be willing to have fun together too. But here's the thing: membership of a sports team is not guaranteed. Players can be traded, replaced or benched if they are not performing. This creates a healthy internal motivation for every player to keep doing their best, because no one likes to be benched.

Now, before you say, 'But I can't just fire someone because they made a mistake,' let me assure you: I agree. Just like a player doesn't get cut after one bad game or a minor injury, it is the overall attitude and commitment that matters most. As you work through this book, you will probably see changes: changes in yourself, changes in your office atmosphere, maybe even changes in how you run meetings or discuss the company vision. You might start asking more of your team and, in return, you might see them step up. But just like in a sports team when a new coach brings in new methods, there will inevitably be people who resist the change.

That is not a negative reflection on them or on you; it simply confirms they aren't the right fit for the high-performing team you are building. Think of it like a breakup in a romantic relationship — it is rarely the fault of just one person. Often parting ways professionally is necessary for both parties to thrive. This doesn't make you an egomaniacal or selfish leader. It simply means you are clear about what you want and how to get there.

Don't let one naysayer drain the energy of a motivated team that is excited to grow. Your team is not your family. It is more like a sports team: if someone is unhappy about the training methods or the way the coach communicates and they keep complaining to their teammates without addressing the issue directly, they will, at best, be moved to the bench or, at worst, be removed from the team entirely. Take the sports coach approach: focus on the star players and those with the right attitude. Put the rest on the bench if needed. In the game of business, you want to play with the best players you have available.

#6: Clear roles lead to clear results

It might sound like common sense, but too many businesses suffer from fuzzy job descriptions, overlapping responsibilities and the dreaded 'that's not my job' mentality. When team members aren't sure what's expected of them, it's a recipe for confusion, frustration and wasted time. But here's the thing: when roles are clear, results follow.

Let's talk numbers for a second. Research from Gallup shows that only 50% of employees know what is expected of them at work,[14] which means half your team could be guessing what they're supposed to be doing every day — not exactly the kind of clarity you need to achieve your business goals, is it? When roles are clearly defined, accountability naturally follows. If everyone knows who is responsible for what, there's no room for finger-pointing or passing the buck. Employees who understand the scope and limits of their roles gain a sense of autonomy and are more likely to take responsibility for their actions (or lack thereof). This, in turn, leads to greater engagement and accountability. When your team members know exactly what's expected of them, they can focus their energy on delivering results instead of second-guessing their tasks. The result? A more focused, motivated and efficient team that drives your business forward.

#7: You can't measure what you don't define

If you don't clearly define what success looks like, how will you know when you've actually achieved it? It's just like setting off on a road trip without a destination — it can be fun and you might cover a lot of ground, but you won't know if you're getting closer to where you want to be. In business, vague goals lead to vague results. When you get clear on your metrics, you create a roadmap that turns your goals into actionable, measurable outcomes.

If you've ever found yourself frustrated by missed targets, unmet expectations or projects that just didn't go the way you wanted them to, the root cause may not be a lack of effort, but instead a lack of clarity. You can't improve what you don't measure, and you can't measure what you don't define. In fact, research highlights the powerful impact of setting clear performance metrics. According to a Gartner study, aligning employee goals with both organisational and individual needs can boost employee performance by up to 22%.[15]

Here's where it gets really interesting: clearly defined metrics do not just improve performance but also employee morale. Gallup's research shows that employees who are actively involved in goal setting are 3.6 times more likely to be engaged at work.[16] When people know what they're working towards and why it matters, they are more motivated, focused and satisfied.

So if you've never set goals for your team in the past, this might be make all the difference. Start by defining your goals and what success looks like and then be specific. Instead of saying 'We need to make more sales', pick a specific number. Are you aiming for a 20% increase? Do you want a certain number of new clients? The clearer the goal, the easier it will be to measure progress. As John Doerr says in his bestselling book *Measure What Matters*, 'If everything is a priority, then nothing is,' so ensure you focus on the objectives that matter most. In your business, this means avoiding shiny object syndrome and instead homing in on the areas that make the biggest difference to your bottom line. By focusing on just a handful of well-defined goals, you can achieve more with less.

Not every metric is actually worth tracking. Focus on the ones that directly impact your bottom line. If your goal, for example, is to improve sales, track metrics like the number of new clients, average sale per transaction, etc. Setting your metrics is not a one-off task. Regularly review your progress, and if something isn't working, readjust. If it is working, do more of it. Remember, you can't manage what you don't measure, and you can't measure what you don't define. So set clear targets, define success and watch your results improve.

#8: Switch off and be present

Being present isn't just about physically showing up — it's about giving your undivided attention to the task or person in front of you. Whether you are deep in strategic planning or having a conversation with a team member, presence requires focus and intention. When you allow yourself to be fully engaged in the moment, you send a powerful message: *this matters and you matter.*

In today's fast-paced, always-on world, distractions are everywhere. Studies have shown that multitasking can reduce productivity by as much as 40% and lead to poorer work quality.[17] The same study has shown that you can only be thinking about one thing at a time and you can only be conducting one mental activity at a time. This means you can either be talking *or* listening, typing *or* reading — one thing at a time. Being present means:

- Turning off notifications or letting your team know you need uninterrupted time when doing strategic work.
- Putting away your phone during one-on-one conversations to show respect and active engagement.
- Stopping the habit of 'half listening' while mentally running through your to-do list.

When you are present, you're not just more productive, you're also more empathetic and approachable. Your team will feel valued, and you will encourage stronger connections. So next time you sit down to work or speak with a team member, try this: pause, breathe and give your full attention. It's a small change that creates a big impact.

Claudia D **THOMPSON**

3. Survey the Current Reality

Whooooweeee! You've done it! Well, at least I hope you've done it. If not, I strongly recommend you go back to Chapter 2 and complete the exercises. This is important stuff. Skipping exercises can say a lot about you. Where else in your life does this show up? Are there other things you only do half-heartedly? Do you often ignore other people's well-meant advice that could help you? Do you then wonder why nothing changes? As Albert Einstein famously put it, doing the same thing over and over again while expecting different results is the very definition of insanity. And that's not how progress happens.

Even though you're an expert in your field and know your business better than anyone else, it doesn't mean you have all the answers. In fact, thinking you already know everything is a surefire way to close yourself off to learning and trying new things, which — surprise, surprise — brings us right back to the definition of insanity. So if you haven't done the exercises in Chapters 1 and 2, I urge you to go back and complete them, otherwise the following chapters won't hold much meaning for you. All right, now we've got that out of the way, where were we?

Having some form of structure in place is crucial, as we explored in Chapter 2. But finding the right balance between an organisational system that supports your team without annoying or frustrating your best and most capable people and one that gives enough support to those who might need a bit more help is the challenge you're facing. The truth is, great people often don't need rigid systems. They are self-motivated and naturally know the right thing to do, but let's be honest, probably not *all* your team members meet those criteria, do they? You probably already have a hunch about who falls into which camp, but this chapter will take the guesswork out of the equation.

It's time to take a deeper look at your current reality. Who are you really working with? Do you have the right people in the right roles? What do they need to shine? In this chapter, we will assess your individual team members, clarify the current role distribution, gather their input and map out any gaps that need addressing. By the end, you will have a clearer picture of where your team stands, and you'll have the basis to create a plan to get everyone aligned and performing at their best.

Who are you working with?

People are different. That is an indisputable fact. Yet I am often amazed by how little understanding and empathy I see when I speak to business owners and staff alike. Many workplaces operate as if everyone should think, act and be motivated in the same way. The truth is, your team is made up of individuals with diverse backgrounds, personalities and preferences.

In this section, we take a closer look at the most common differences between people — their ages, personality types and what drives them. By recognising and accommodating these differences, you can reduce conflicts and improve team dynamics and productivity. Understanding how each of your team members ticks is not just a nice-to-have, it's a must-have. It allows you to assign tasks more strategically, create an inclusive work environment and support your team by playing to their individual strengths. When you leverage this knowledge, you are not just managing people, you are empowering them to perform at their best.

While it's crucial to understand your team members' personalities, it's just as important to recognise that not all differences are set in stone. Personality traits are relatively stable over time — for example, whether someone is naturally introverted or extroverted or how they approach a problem. On the other hand, behavioural differences can be influenced by the work environment, the company culture and even the task at hand. For example, a team member might be more detail-oriented in a high-pressure project but more relaxed and creative in brainstorming sessions.

Understanding the unique mix of personalities and behaviours within your team is only the first step. The real power lies in applying this knowledge to create a more effective and harmonious work environment. For instance, assigning detail-oriented projects to your more analytical team members while allowing creative thinkers to brainstorm solutions can lead to better outcomes. The goal is not to change who your team members are but to make use of their unique strengths.

Different generations in the workplace

An average employee works up to 50 years of their life. It is no surprise, then, that people of all ages come together in the workplace — people who might not naturally mingle outside the office. In the following pages I have put together an overview of the current generations in the workplace and what makes them tick.

Baby boomers (born between 1946 and 1964) – the workhorses
Baby boomers represent the 76 million people born during the post-World War II baby boom. In 2023 they made up about 17% of the global workforce.

What they value:

- **Work ethic**: They value hard work, loyalty and a strong work ethic. Many of them are highly dedicated to their roles and prefer in-person work environments.
- **Stability**: They appreciate job security and stable benefits. They often value long-term career growth within the same company.
- **Recognition**: Baby boomers value being recognised for their experience and contributions. They often define themselves through their work achievements, and they are often very competitive.

What annoys them:
- **Lack of respect**: They can be annoyed by a perceived lack of respect from younger generations or by being disregarded as 'outdated'.
- **Change**: Rapid technological changes can be frustrating if they are not supported by adequate training.
- **Informality**: Casual attitudes in the workplace, especially towards authority, may irritate them.

How to best manage them:
- **Respect experience**: Acknowledge and respect their experience and knowledge. Involve them in mentoring roles.
- **Offer stability**: Highlight the stability and long-term perspective of the job, while encouraging adaptability to new technology with the appropriate training.
- **Clear communication**: Provide clear, direct communication and set expectations.
- **Give instructions, not debates**: Baby boomers tend to accept the chain of command and often comply without further discussion. They appreciate clear directives and are less likely to push back on decisions.

Generation X (born between 1965 and 1980) – the independents
Generation X, often nicknamed the 'middle child', is sandwiched between baby boomers and millennials. They currently make up about 33% of the global workforce.

What they value:
- **Work–life balance**: Gen Xers are the first generation to start focusing on a life outside work. They value work–life balance and flexibility in their work arrangements.
- **Autonomy**: They prefer to work independently and appreciate autonomy in their roles.
- **Efficiency**: They value efficiency and practicality, often seeking the most effective ways to do things.

What annoys them:
- **Micromanagement**: They dislike being micromanaged and prefer to be trusted to do their jobs.
- **Lack of flexibility**: Rigid work environments without flexibility in hours or locations.
- **Inefficiency**: Bureaucracy and unnecessary meetings are seen as timewasters.

How to best manage them:
- **Offer flexibility**: Provide opportunities for flexible hours or remote work.
- **Empowerment**: Give them autonomy in their roles, allowing them to make decisions and manage their work.
- **Practical support**: Focus on efficiency in processes and tools. Be straightforward in communication.
- **Autonomy**: They value a hands-off and autonomous management style.

Millennials/Generation Y (born between 1981 and 1996) – the purpose-seekers

Millennials reached adulthood around the time of the millennium. They arrived in the workplace at the same time as the internet, and they are technology natives. They are already the largest group in the workforce and are projected to make up 75% of the global workforce by 2030.

What they value:
- **Purpose**: Millennials seek purpose in their work and want to feel they are making a difference.
- **Development**: They value opportunities for professional development, learning and career progression.
- **Flexibility and work–life integration:** Like Gen X, they value work–life balance but also want work–life integration, where they can blend personal and professional life seamlessly.

What annoys them:
- **Lack of feedback:** Millennials often seek regular feedback and can be frustrated by infrequent communication.
- **Inflexibility:** They dislike rigid structures that don't allow for flexibility or creativity.
- **Slow career progression:** Millennials can become disengaged if they feel their career progression is too slow or unclear.

How to best manage them:
- **Provide regular feedback:** Offer continuous feedback and recognition for their work.
- **Career development**: Create clear paths for advancement and provide opportunities for skill development.
- **Encourage collaboration:** Promote a collaborative work environment where ideas and creativity are valued.
- **Teamwork:** They prefer a teamwork approach over authoritative management.

Gen Z (born between 1997 and 2012) – the digital natives
Gen Z is the first generation to grow up without any recollection of a world without the internet. Having witnessed financial crises and seen the impact of work stress on their parents, they are determined to avoid making the same mistakes.

What they value:
- **Digital connectivity**: As true digital natives, they expect seamless integration of technology in their work.
- **Diversity and inclusion**: They are passionate about diversity, inclusion and social responsibility. They see teamwork as the driver for organisational innovation.
- **Entrepreneurial spirit**: They often value creativity, side projects and roles that allow for entrepreneurial thinking.

What annoys them?
- **Outdated technology**: They can become frustrated with slow or outdated technology and processes.
- **Inflexibility**: A disregard for their individual needs for time off or flexible working can be off-putting.
- **Hierarchical structures**: Traditional, top-down structures that limit their ability to voice opinions or affect change can be discouraging.

How to best manage them:
- **Flexibility**: Allow for hybrid working arrangements and flexible hierarchies.
- **Focus on wellbeing**: Provide resources that support mental and physical health.
- **Make it fun**: Encourage innovative thinking, continuous learning and career development.
- **Human-first approach**: Communicate clearly with a personalised touch.

In recent years, Gen Z, in particular, has developed a reputation for being 'entitled' in the workplace. But let's not forget — every generation has faced criticism from the one before. Different values don't mean different generations can't work together or achieve great results. The key lies in understanding what drives each group and leveraging their unique strengths to build cohesive, high-performing teams.

While employers have expressed dissatisfaction, citing a lack of preparedness and unrealistic work demands,[18] and six in ten Gen Z employees are reportedly let go within their first year — often due to challenges with communication, feedback and aligning expectations[19] — this generation also brings a deep passion for work—life balance, mental health and flexible environments. Rather than dismiss these differences, I see them as a call to action. By creating workplaces that prioritise open communication, support and clear expectations, we can unlock the potential of this highly motivated and innovative group. When we embrace these challenges, we don't just help Gen Z — we strengthen our teams and workplaces as a whole.

DISC: Understanding your team's personalities

There are endless personality assessment tools available to help you understand yourself and your team. Each has its own benefits and limitations. Personally, I am a big fan of the DISC model for its simplicity, extensive usability and timeless relevance. This model is a widely recognised framework for understanding human behaviour and personality traits. It was developed by psychologist William Moulton Marston in the 1920s and categorises personalities into four primary types, represented by the letters D, I, S and C.

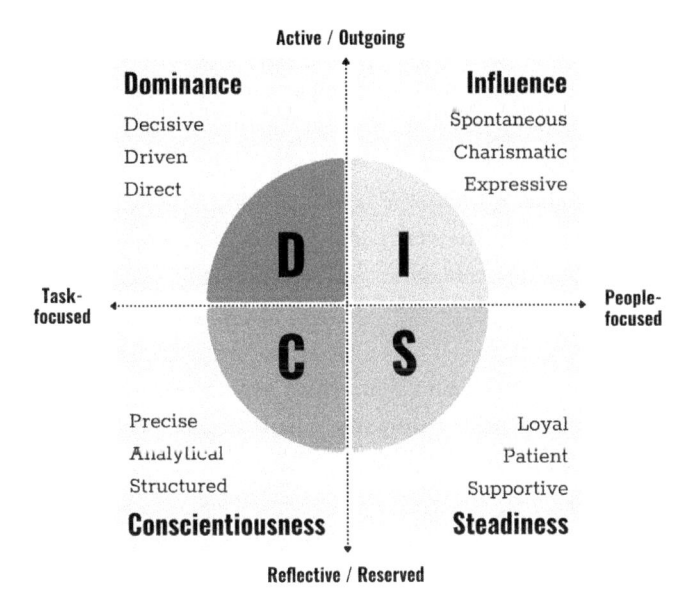

```
                    Active / Outgoing
         Dominance         │      Influence
         Decisive          │      Spontaneous
         Driven            │      Charismatic
         Direct            │      Expressive
                      D    │    I
Task-  ←──────────────────────────────────────→  People-
focused                    │                       focused
                      C    │    S
         Precise           │      Loyal
         Analytical        │      Patient
         Structured        │      Supportive
         Conscientiousness │      Steadiness
                    Reflective / Reserved
```

While many people exhibit a mix of these types, some combinations are more common than others. Around 40% of individuals tend to be S types or S combinations, followed by I types at about 30%. C types make up around 20% and D types are the rarest, representing only about 10% of the population. The model gained further popularity through Thomas Erikson, who simplified it by using colours: red for D, yellow for I, green for S and blue for C. For a deeper dive into his system, I highly recommend his book *Surrounded by Idiots*.

How can you identify DISC profiles?
You might be wondering how to recognise DISC profiles in your team. While the most reliable method is through an official assessment, there are clues you can pick up in everyday interactions.

In conversations:
> **D (Dominance)**: Brief, straightforward and often forceful. They focus on actions and outcomes; and tend to skip pleasantries.

I (Influence): Enthusiastic and expressive, their conversations resemble a one-person show filled with ups and downs. Expect detours and animated storytelling.

S (Steadiness): Their stories will be about other people and who they were with. They take their time to ensure you are following along. They are thoughtful and will probably ask how you have been.

C (Conscientiousness): Methodical and detail-focused, they may either be brief or dive deep into minute details. Their tone is more formal and precise.

In emails:

D: Quick one-liners that focus only on the most relevant point. Quite likely to forget the attachment.

I: Emails filled with emojis, exclamation marks and expressive language. Most likely to forget the attachment.

S: Polite, considerate and detailed, often mentioning the team.

C: Thorough, structured and comprehensive, often including attachments or links for further detail.

In meetings:

> **D**: Takes charge, pushes for action steps and gets straight to the point.
>
> **I**: Loves brainstorming and group participation and often goes off on tangents with enthusiasm.
>
> **S**: Patient and supportive, they ensure everyone is heard and avoid confrontation.
>
> **C**: Focuses on verifying facts, data and details with a calm and methodical approach.

Now you have an idea of how to recognise different DISC profiles, here's a quick reference guide to help you understand their strengths, needs and preferred communication styles.

DISC type	Dominance (D)	Influence (I)	Steadiness (S)	Conscientiousness (C)
Focus	Task-focused, fast, outgoing	People-focused, fast, outgoing	People-focused, considered, reserved	Task-focused, reserved, passive
Attributes	**Positive:** Strong-willed, independent, ambitious **Can seem:** Pushy, tough, dominant	**Positive:** Inspiring, enthusiastic, outgoing **Can seem:** Hot tempered, undisciplined	**Positive:** Supportive, reliable, respectful **Can seem:** Stubborn, indecisive	**Positive:** Diligent, methodical, thoughtful **Can seem:** critical, narrow-minded, overly detailed
Strength	Problem-solver	Encourager	Supporter	Organiser
Conflict response	Demands, may become dictatorial	Attacks, may become sarcastic	Complies, may become submissive	Avoids, may become withdrawn
Motivated by	Challenging tasks, power, competition	Social recognition, group activities	Stable environments, appreciation	Structured tasks, order, quality
Dislikes	Losing, inefficiency	Rejection, boredom	Sudden change, conflict	Being wrong, lack of preparation
Best-suited jobs	Team leaders, sales, operations	PR, sales, creative director	Customer service, HR, executive assistant	Engineering, finance, analysis
Perfect meetings	Brief, to the point	In person, without rigid agenda	Prepared agenda, in person or online	Formally scheduled, with detailed agenda
Perfect emails	Brief, to the point	Friendly, personal, clear call to action	Warm, clear, informative	Detailed, factual, with supporting documents

Understanding your team's DISC profiles is only half the story. The other half is using that knowledge to refine your leadership. No DISC profile is inherently better than another; each brings unique strengths to the table. A team full of decisive D types might be great for quick decisions but may struggle with empathy and collaboration. On the other hand, a group dominated by steady S types is fantastic for stability and harmony but could lack the drive for innovation. The key to success lies in balancing your team with the right mix of DISC profiles, ensuring each person is in a role that plays to their strengths while addressing potential blind spots.

Tips for leading based on your own DISC profile

Equally important is knowing your own DISC profile and how it influences your leadership style. Your natural tendencies — whether taking charge, supporting others, focusing on details or innovating — will impact how you show up for your team, make decisions and handle challenges. By understanding your own DISC traits, you can not only leverage your strengths but also address areas where you may need to adapt. Leadership is as much about self-awareness as it is about team dynamics. With this in mind, here are some practical tips tailored to help bosses of each DISC type lead their team more effectively.

Dominant boss (D):
- Listen to others' opinions, involve your team in decisions and give clear instructions.
- Be patient; your innate urgency may cause stress.
- Spend one-on-one time with team members who need it.
- Give sufficient warning before implementing major changes.

Influencing boss (I):
- Focus on planning and prioritising: follow through on one idea at a time.
- Stay organised — tidy up your workspace and focus on task completion.

- Limit socialising during work hours and give others a chance to speak.
- Avoid making impulsive decisions based on gut feelings.

Steady boss (S):
- Be more assertive and direct in difficult conversations (use the FAB framework set out in BOSS fact #4).
- Take charge when needed, especially during decision making.
- Prepare for change and learn to adapt quickly.
- Don't shy away from giving constructive feedback.

Conscientious boss (C):
- Seek workable solutions instead of perfect ones.
- Avoid micromanaging; set clear expectations upfront and trust your team.
- Be open to alternative approaches and diverse problem-solving methods.
- Focus on people, not just processes — take time to understand different viewpoints.

This overview is just a starting point for understanding the different personalities in your workplace. Hopefully you have recognised yourself or your team members in these descriptions. Maybe you have even had an *aha* moment when you realised someone struggled because they were assigned a task that didn't align with their DISC profile. If you are interested in exploring this further, understanding mixed types or discovering your precise DISC profile, head over to www.takecharge-thebook.com.

Motivators and other differentiators

In addition to different personalities, your team members also have individual motivators and working styles. It's important to note that you can't simply tell someone to 'work harder' and expect them to be motivated. Instead, you need to uncover what truly drives them and find ways to ensure they receive those rewards in exchange for good performance.

Motivators can be divided into two main categories: extrinsic and intrinsic. Extrinsic motivators include things like compensation, benefits, recognition, rewards, job security and work environment. Intrinsic motivators, on the other hand, are more about purpose, meaning, autonomy, mastery and growth opportunities. According to various studies by the International Journal of Environmental Research and Public Health,[20] Deloitte,[21] McKinsey and Company,[22] and PwC,[23] motivators can vary based on factors like age, gender and cultural background, but it's essential not to make assumptions or fall into the stereotype trap.

For example, while some individuals may find financial rewards and career advancement highly motivating, others may prioritise recognition, collaboration or roles that offer personal growth and purpose. These preferences often transcend traditional categories and are shaped by personal values, experiences and career stages. By taking the time to understand each team member's unique motivators — rather than relying on generalisations — you can create a more engaged and fulfilled workforce.

While there are no rigid rules about which demographic is motivated by what, three key areas can give you clues:

1. Their personal lives. What do they do outside work? What are their hobbies?
2. Their DISC profile (see table on page 114).
3. The tasks they naturally gravitate towards. What do they volunteer for? What are they exceptionally good at?

Now let's put a stubborn myth to rest: the idea that simply increasing someone's salary makes them more motivated or likely to stay longer.

117

This is not true! Employees want to be happy in their jobs. They want to feel valued, appreciated and challenged. In fact, more than half the participants in a 2024 Ford Motor Co. study reported that they would be willing to take a 20% pay cut for a better work—life balance.[24] But that's not all: the largest study of its kind, which analysed real-world data from over 200,000 US public sector employees, found that workers who are intrinsically motivated are three times more engaged than those focused solely on extrinsic rewards.[25] And here's the kicker: money often encourages short-term, self-serving behaviours but does little to inspire lasting engagement or commitment to the organisation. So let's finally put that myth to bed and focus on understanding what truly motivates each individual on your team to love what they do.

Beyond their motivators, your team members also have different working styles. Understanding these can help you match employees to roles and work environments where they can excel. Here are a few common styles:

- independent vs collaborative
- analytical vs intuitive
- detail-oriented vs big-picture
- structured vs flexible
- proactive vs reactive
- task-oriented vs people-oriented
- extroverted vs introverted
- in-person vs remote working.

For example, a detail-oriented, structured person might feel right at home in accounting but overwhelmed in a fast-paced operations role that requires quick reactions. Someone who is more task- than people-oriented might not be best suited for a customer service role. A big-picture, flexible individual might excel at strategic planning, where thinking outside the box is an asset.

If you've made it this far and are starting to realise that improving team dynamics might be a bit more complex than hosting a one-day team-building event followed by pizza for everyone, then congratulations —

you are exactly where you need to be. But don't worry! It might feel overwhelming right now, but the good news is that the upcoming chapters will guide you step by step through the process of making sustainable changes.

Yes, we will rock the boat — but not so hard it capsizes! Think of it like taking your boat out of the water and turning it over to fix a few holes before pushing it back in. And if, during that process, you find your boat is too rusty to repair, then maybe it's time to reach out for help. Head over to www.takecharge-thebook.com if you're feeling stuck or need support. Sometimes being too close to the boat — or being tied down by your own baggage — can cloud your thinking. I am here to help you and your team get back on course.

Exercise: Who is on your team?
60 minutes

Take some time to individually assess each team member. Use the questions below to create a detailed profile for each person, based on your observations and interactions and any insights you gained from the DISC profiles, motivators and generational differences. The goal of this exercise is to get a clearer understanding of who you are working with so you can better align their roles with their natural strengths, provide tailored support for their professional growth and help them improve their productivity.

Consider this an opportunity to step back and view your team holistically while focusing on each person as an individual. What are their unique skills and talents? What motivates them to do their best work? Where are they struggling? How can you help them succeed? By reflecting on these and the following questions, you will gain valuable insights, which we'll need for upcoming chapters.

> Remember, this exercise isn't about labelling your team members or placing them in rigid categories. It's about using what you've learned to make thoughtful, informed decisions that benefit both the individual and the team as a whole.
>
> - What do they excel at? Understanding their strengths will help you assign tasks that they will thrive in.
> - What have they struggled with in the past? Identifying challenges allows you to provide more targeted support.
> - What are they known for in the office? Are they popular? This helps assess their impact on team dynamics and morale.
> - Do customers or suppliers mention them? For good or bad reasons? This gives an outside perspective on what they stand out for.
> - What is their attitude like towards change and innovation? This will help you understand how they might react to shifts in strategy or new initiatives.
> - Are they creative? Knowing this can help in getting them involved in tasks that require out-of-the-box thinking.
> - Have a guess at their DISC profile. This will help you tailor your communication and management style.

Understanding the different DISC profiles, generations and motivators within your team is not just an intellectual exercise — it's a practical tool to help you become a better boss and create a more cohesive, productive workplace. By creating detailed profiles for your team members, you have taken the first step towards identifying patterns that will guide your leadership. Who is thriving in their current role? Who might perform even better in a different position? Are there recurring challenges stemming from mismatched roles, communication gaps or a lack of diversity of personalities? As you move forward, use these reflections to:

- tailor your leadership style to meet individual needs,
- align roles with each person's strengths and motivators,
- improve communication and collaboration,
- identify opportunities for growth and development, and
- build a team with diverse, complementary personalities.

Over the next few weeks, pay close attention to your team's behaviours, motivators and interactions. Make notes about what stands out to you. As with all the changes in this book, start small, perhaps adapting your communication style with one or two team members and observing the results. Remember, this is a gradual process. Your goal is not to transform everything overnight but to develop deeper insights that allow you to lead with intention and flexibility. That said, if you are reading this and thinking, "I don't have weeks. I want to change things NOW!", there's a pretty good chance you're a high D or I personality. If that sounds like you, take a deep breath and refer back to the tips a few pages ago where we covered tips to help you balance your natural urgency with a more sustainable approach. Ultimately, by understanding the unique personalities within your business, you move beyond merely managing tasks. You become a leader who genuinely connects with the people behind the work.

What are they doing?

Before we look at whether your team members hold the right roles, let's take a step back and get everything that needs to be done in your business out of your head and onto paper.

Many business owners assume they have a clear picture of the work required to keep the business running. However, when asked to write it all down, they often realise there are hidden tasks, inefficiencies and even entire areas of responsibility that haven't been deliberately assigned.

The following exercise will help you create a comprehensive bird's-eye view of everything that needs to happen in your business to keep it running smoothly. Later, when we map out your organisational structure, this list will serve as a foundation for ensuring that nothing falls through the cracks.

Exercise: What needs to get done?
60 minutes

Step 1: The big brain dump

Find a blank sheet of paper, open a spreadsheet or use a whiteboard — whatever helps you think most freely. Now write down every single task that your business requires to function. Don't worry about who does what — just focus on capturing everything.

To make sure you don't miss anything, break your business down into functional areas and consider:

Daily operations (the core work)
- What needs to happen every day to keep the business running?
- What do you deliver to customers or clients?
- What processes ensure smooth fulfilment of products or services?
- What admin tasks keep things moving (emails, scheduling, etc.)?

Sales and marketing (bringing in business)
- How do you generate leads or attract customers?
- What marketing activities are in place (social media, email campaigns, SEO, paid ads)?
- What sales processes need to be followed?

Purchasing and procurement (keeping supplies stocked)
- What products or materials do you need to buy regularly for the business?
- How do you manage supplier relationships, ordering and stock levels?
- Are there contracts or agreements with suppliers that need maintaining?
- Do you have a process for negotiating better deals or finding new suppliers?

Office and facilities management (keeping the workplace running smoothly)
- What is required for the office or workspace to be functional?
- What needs to be handled for cleaning, maintenance and general upkeep?
- How are office supplies replenished (stationery, coffee, snacks, etc.)?

IT and technology (keeping systems running)
- What software, tools or systems does the business rely on daily?
- What is required for IT security, backups and troubleshooting?
- What happens when tech issues arise?

Finance (keeping the money flowing)
- What needs to happen to ensure money comes in on time?
- How do you handle expenses, payroll and budgeting?
- What financial tracking and reporting are necessary?

People and team management (keeping the team engaged)
- What tasks involve hiring, onboarding and training?
- How do you handle team meetings?

Strategy and growth (moving the business forward)
- What planning or goal-setting activities are required?
- What partnerships or networking efforts are necessary?
- What innovations, product developments or expansions are being worked on?

If you are struggling to come up with everything, try walking through a typical workday or week in your business. What do you and your team do from morning until the end of the day? What seasonal or annual tasks pop up that aren't part of the daily grind?

Step 2: Organise your task list

Now that you have everything out of your head, let's structure it:

1. Sort your list into categories. Use the functional areas above as a guide.
2. Break down broad tasks into smaller steps (for example, instead of just writing 'Social Media', specify what that includes, e.g. content creation, posting, engagement, analytics tracking, etc.).
3. Identify recurring versus one-off tasks. Mark whether each task is daily, weekly, monthly or occasional.

> Once completed, the list will serve as a central reference point that we'll return to when we analyse whether the right people are in the right positions and when we map out your organisational structure later on. Beyond helping you get clarity, this list is a powerful tool when talking to your team members about what they are responsible for, assigning clear ownership of tasks and responsibilities, delegating more effectively to give your team members more autonomy and freeing up your time as a boss so you can focus more on the things you *want* to work on. But we're getting ahead of ourselves. For now, don't worry about *who* does what, just focus on making sure everything is accounted for.

Now that you have a clear view of what needs to get done, it's time to take a step back and ask yourself: do I have the right people on the bus? And perhaps even more importantly, are they in the right seats? If you're wondering why I'm suddenly talking about a bus, let me explain. The concept of 'first who, then what' (using the bus analogy) was popularised by Jim Collins in his book *Good to Great*. The idea is that as a business owner, you should first ensure you're working with great people before deciding what you want them to do.

If you have the right people on the bus, it almost doesn't matter where the bus is going. As long as the people around you share your values and have the right attitude, they'll be a tremendous asset to your business, even if you aren't entirely sure where the business is headed. But it's not just about hiring (and retaining) talented individuals, it's about aligning their roles with what they are naturally good at and passionate about. When you have the right people in the right seats, your business becomes more efficient, agile and resilient. However, if someone is in the wrong seat, it doesn't just affect their performance — it can drag down the morale and productivity of the entire team. So let's get into the exercise to help you determine whether each team member is in the right role and whether they should even be on the bus at all.

Exercise: Right people, right seat
30 minutes

Look at your list of team members you made for the 'Who is on your team?' exercise earlier and rate every person on the following seven factors using this rating scale. You can find a template to use on www.takecharge-thebook.com.

1 = needs significant improvement
2 = below average
3 = meets expectations
4 = above average
5 = excellent

Factor	Name 1	Name 2	Name 3	Name 4
Engagement and motivation How motivated and engaged is this team member? Are they proactive or do they seem disengaged?				
Performance and results Is this team member consistently meeting or exceeding expectations? Do they deliver the results you expect from their position?				
Cultural fit and values alignment Does this person fit well with your company culture? Are they aligned with your business's core values?				
Adaptability and growth potential Do they adapt to challenges? Can they grow in this role and take on more responsibility?				

Factor	Name 1	Name 2	Name 3	Name 4
Job satisfaction Does this person express satisfaction with their role? How long do you think they will stay with the company?				
Natural strengths and passions Does the role tap into their natural strengths? Are they thriving because the job aligns with their abilities?				
Skill alignment Does this person have the skills and experience needed for their current role? Are they efficient in executing their tasks?				
TOTAL				

The categories above allow you to evaluate your team members on their general attitude, how well they fit into the company and their suitability for their current role. The maximum score possible is 35. The lowest score is 7. Team members scoring 27 and above are likely to be the right people in the right seats. For those with scores in the mid-range between 15 and 26, pay attention to the specific areas where they scored poorly, as these might indicate a need for further discussion, training or reassignment.

- Are they currently in the best role for their skills and strengths?
- How can you leverage their strengths better within your team?
- What areas do they need more support in and how can you provide it?
- Are there any team dynamics that need adjusting or addressing based on what you have discovered?

> Anyone with a score below 14 is probably not the right person for your bus and may require a difficult conversation about their future in the company. If you're still unsure about someone, here's a simple test. Would you hire them again knowing everything you know now? If the answer is no, that's a clear indication they may not be the best fit for your organisation.

The organisational structure

Now we have examined whether you have the right people in the right seats, let's take a closer look at the organisational structure you currently have in place. Even if you don't have a formal structure, some sort of hierarchy and distribution of roles has probably developed organically — often influenced by factors such as length of service, age, task preferences and even how much you enjoy interacting with certain team members.

Unlike the 'ideal hierarchy' exercise in Chapter 2, which focuses on envisioning the future structure that aligns with your goals, this exercise is about mapping the current reality of how roles and responsibilities are distributed. By understanding your existing structure, you can identify what is working, where inefficiencies exist and how it compares to your ideal vision. This analysis will serve as a crucial foundation for bridging the gap between where you are and where you want to be.

Exercise: Mapping your organisational structure
30 minutes

Step 1: Start by gathering any existing documents that outline roles, job descriptions or team structures, plus the list of tasks on page 74. If you don't have any formal documents yet, use what you can find or recall. (Note: because this is very important, you and your team will write a clear job description in the form of a positional contract in Chapter 4 [page 176.)

Step 2: Write down all the current roles in your business. For each role, specify:
- title
- key responsibilities (using your task list and job descriptions)
- who they report to
- who currently occupies the role.

Step 3: Assign the tasks identified on page 74 to each role until all tasks are accounted for. Identify any responsibilities that have emerged organically but that are not (yet) formally recognised. Are there any overlaps where multiple team members are handling the same tasks?

Step 4: Create an organisational chart that visually represents your current hierarchy. Start with top management and work your way down until everyone is accounted for.

Once you've mapped out your current organisational structure, take some time to reflect on the following questions about your structure:

- How close is the actual structure to the ideal one you designed in Chapter 2?
- Does the current structure support your business goals?
- Is the current structure scalable as the business grows or will it need adjustments?
- Does it make sense? Are there any roles that seem redundant or outdated?
- Are there any informal lines of authority or influence that don't appear on the chart but are important in practice?
- Are there any barriers or bottlenecks that slow down decision making or communication?
- Should any roles, responsibilities or reporting lines be redefined?

With this exercise, you will gain valuable insights into whether your current setup is supporting your future growth. It's not just about putting names in boxes but ensuring the structure you have in place empowers your team to shine and aligns with where your business is headed. This sets you up perfectly for the next step: gathering feedback from your team to get their perspective on how things in the business are working for them.

Getting their perspective

You have done a lot of reflection by now. You've mapped out your vision for the business, assessed your current team and started to gain clarity about where things need to go. But here's the truth: no matter how much you observe or analyse your team, there are insights you simply won't uncover unless you *ask them*. And that's where the next part of the process comes in.

Think of this next part as putting a stethoscope to your business's heartbeat. It's a way to measure the health of your organisation by hearing directly from your people. While you might feel confident that you know your team, they may have thoughts, feelings or frustrations they have never felt comfortable sharing. This is not because they are secretive or difficult but because vulnerability in a professional setting is tough, especially when it involves speaking up to the boss.

We will get your team's feedback in two ways: an anonymous survey and individual interviews. An anonymous survey offers a safe space for honesty. It gives every team member a voice, no matter how introverted, shy or cautious they may be. It's the first step towards truly understanding the reality of your workplace. In the individual interviews you get to ask questions and learn more.

Why does this matter? Because what you don't know can hurt you. Without understanding your team's true engagement levels, the dynamics of your team and the challenges your employees face every day, you risk making assumptions, implementing changes that miss the mark or overlooking small issues that could escalate into major problems. Gathering your team's feedback is especially crucial in today's market, where employees' expectations are shifting. Attracting and retaining the right talent hinges on making sure your people feel heard, valued and supported for success.

Asking for feedback should not be a tick box exercise. Your team won't willingly share their thoughts if they feel their input just disappears into a black hole every time. According to the State of Employee Feedback 2021 survey by AllVoices, 41% of employees have left a job because they didn't feel listened to.[26] I don't know about you, but I certainly have. You can only contribute ideas unheard for so long before you stop trying. So remember, gathering input in the first place and making changes based on it is how you build trust and loyalty.

This is your opportunity to demonstrate that you care about your employees' experiences and that their feedback will shape the future of the company. By asking the right questions and committing to action, you can create a foundation of trust, align your team's efforts with your goals and make meaningful, lasting improvements to your workplace culture.

Step 1: An anonymous engagement survey

Gathering your team's honest input is the first step to understanding where things stand. You are setting a baseline for their current engagement levels. This survey will allow your team to share their thoughts openly, without fear of repercussions, and help you pinpoint areas for improvement. On www.takecharge-thebook.com you have two options to get you started:

1. **Manual process**: Download a printable form to use with your team. This option allows you to work through the survey manually, adding scores yourself. It's a great way to engage directly with the data and get hands-on insights into your team's feedback.
2. **Interactive online tool:** We are continually improving an interactive online survey tool that simplifies the process and allows an even more detailed look into the goings-on in your workplace. It automatically compiles responses, calculates engagement scores and highlights key trends. As this tool is ever evolving to provide the best insights for both bosses and teams, check the website for the latest version.

Whether you choose the manual or online method, the process is straightforward.

Explain the survey

Let your team know what the survey is for. Emphasise that their feedback is completely anonymous (especially if using the online tool) and that it will be used to improve the workplace, not to single anyone out. Assure them that their honesty is valued and essential for driving positive change.

Share the survey

Provide a printed copy of the manual option or share the online link with your team. Give clear instructions on how to complete it and set a deadline for responses to ensure timely feedback.

Survey structure

The (manual) survey consists of 20 quick questions grouped into various topics, rated on a scale of 1 (strongly disagree) to 5 (strongly agree). Questions cover key areas like team dynamics, management communication, job satisfaction and alignment with company goals.

Collect and compile

For the manual version, collect completed surveys and calculate the engagement score yourself using the instructions provided in the downloadable template. For the online tool, the platform will handle the calculations and generate your engagement score automatically.

Review your baseline

The resulting score provides a numerical benchmark for your team's current engagement levels. This will be your reference point for tracking progress as you implement changes.

Once all responses have been compiled, whether manually or through the online tool, you will receive a numerical engagement score. Here's how to interpret it:

Score below 3: Low engagement — indicates significant issues with motivation, job satisfaction or alignment with the company's goals and culture. Address these areas quickly to prevent declining performance, absenteeism or burnout.

Score between 3 and 4: Moderate engagement — suggests your team is somewhat engaged but probably has areas of dissatisfaction. Use this as an opportunity to target specific improvements and raise overall job satisfaction.

Score above 4: High engagement — great job! Your team is engaged and motivated. Focus on maintaining this momentum, preventing complacency and addressing any emerging challenges.

Remember, engagement levels are not static. As your team evolves, so will their needs, motivators and challenges. Regularly revisiting the engagement survey — whether annually or during significant changes — will ensure that you're staying on top of potential issues and continuously improving your workplace culture.

Step 2: The individual interviews

With the survey results in hand and your new plans for the organisation, it's now time for deeper one-on-one interviews. The goal here is to validate the data, confirm findings from previous exercises and uncover anything that might have been missed. These conversations are where you will get the most actionable insights, but they can also be the most nerve-racking — for both you and your employees. The key here is to approach them with curiosity, openness and empathy. As much as you might be trying to avoid them (I am looking at you, High S and High C personalities), it's important for you personally to do them, and without anyone else present. Creating a two-against-one situation might throw off the natural power imbalance even more, create unnecessary tension and not produce any real valuable feedback.

Setting the stage

When you announce the upcoming interviews, emphasise that these conversations are about building a stronger, more aligned company where everyone can fulfil their full potential and enjoy coming to work. It's important to reassure your team that:

- *Every team member* will be spoken to, to avoid anyone feeling singled out.
- The purpose of these interviews is to understand how to improve the work environment and identify opportunities for growth — not to reprimand anyone.
- Everyone's input is valued, because the company is entering a new phase of growth and their perspectives are crucial to shaping the future.
- The interviews are about listening, not judging. Encourage your team to be open and honest so you can better support them in their roles.
- All interviews will be private, confidential and focused on both the company's growth and their personal development.
- You are committed to using their input to drive positive change.

However, avoid making blanket statements like 'nobody has anything to worry about'. Instead, emphasise that the goal is to create a more effective and enjoyable workplace for everyone. Let them know that feedback is about continuous improvement for both the company and its people, and that you want to better understand their needs and how you can align their strengths with the company's vision and goals.

Scheduling the interviews

When setting up your individual interviews, plan for 30-minute slots but allocate a full hour per interview. Why 30 minutes? Because keeping the conversation focused ensures you cover what truly matters without the discussion drifting into general chit-chat or losing direction. At the same time, blocking out a full hour gives you a buffer for preparation, note-taking and a quick reset between conversations. To stay fresh and engaged, limit yourself to three or four interviews per day. These conversations are a valuable opportunity to understand your team on a deeper level, and they require focus and genuine presence. Cramming too many into one day can lead to fatigue, which makes it harder to give each team member the attention they deserve.

Preparing for the interviews
Before you start the interviews, take some time to prepare yourself mentally. This process is not just about gathering feedback or having potentially difficult conversations; it is about setting the foundation for building a legacy. You are working to create a business that's bigger than you and bigger than its current team. Getting yourself in the right headspace is essential — these interviews are a key step in aligning your team with the vision you've painted for the business. Everyone on your team is welcome to join you on this new journey, but it's important to remember they may almost need to 'requalify' to remain on the bus with you.

Wear your vision, determination and new motivation like armour. As you go into these conversations, remember, nothing bad is going to happen to you. Your family will still love you, your business won't crumble, and standing up for what is important to you doesn't make you a bad person. Even if the conversations are tough or you struggle to find the perfect words, focus on your intention and tone of voice. Remember the communication breakdown we discussed earlier: only 7% of communication is determined by the words you use, while the rest comes from your tone and body language. So don't overthink the specific words. Instead, trust in your preparation and the bigger vision you have for the business. They will carry you through.

Before every interview, look at the notes you made about the team member in previous exercises, their current position and responsibilities, and where you potentially see them in the new structure. Note down any individual questions. It's also important to note that some of your team members, particularly those with S (Steadiness) and C (Conscientiousness) profiles, may prefer to take their time to think through their responses. For these individuals, consider providing a printout or online form with the questions after the conversation. This allows them to reflect and respond in a less pressurised setting. Be sure to set a clear deadline for their responses, though, to avoid unnecessary delays or missing valuable feedback.

Getting ready for productive conversations
Creating the right environment for your interviews is crucial for in putting your team members at ease and encouraging open and honest dialogue. The physical setup of the room can make all the difference: avoid sitting across a desk from your employee. This creates an unnecessary barrier and reinforces the power dynamic. Make sure that *you* as the boss don't sit closest to the door: this positioning can unconsciously signal a desire to leave quickly or can make your team member feel trapped. Let them have the seat closest to the exit to make them feel less confined and more in control.

Provide small comforts to create a welcoming atmosphere: offer tea, coffee, water and maybe even a selection of biscuits or snacks. A small gesture like this can go a long way in making the conversation feel more casual and less formal. Ensure the room is private and free from distractions — silence your phone, unplug any office landlines and inform others not to disturb you during the session. Lastly, be mindful of your body language. Maintain an open posture — no crossed arms or leaning away. Make sure your chair is at the same height as theirs to avoid creating a sense of hierarchy. Begin the conversation with a smile and a friendly tone to help break the ice. These small, thoughtful touches can significantly affect how comfortable your employee feels and how honest and productive the conversation will be. Remember, the goal is to create a relaxed, safe space where team members feel encouraged to share their thoughts openly.

During the conversations, be sure to listen actively and pay close attention to non-verbal cues like their tone, body language and any hesitation in their responses. If they are hesitant or reserved, prompt them with 'what else?' at least three times to dig deeper. Remember, introverted team members may prefer to provide their feedback in writing — offer that option at the end of every interview. Allow yourself time to reset between interviews so you can bring your best energy to each conversation. These interviews are your moment to listen, learn and lead with confidence.

In addition to any individual questions based on your previous findings, also cover the following topics:

- role clarity
- engagement and motivation levels
- current workload and stress levels
- training needs
- team dynamics
- opportunities for improvement.

For a detailed list of questions, head to www.takecharge-thebook.com. Before the end of the interview, ask if there's anything else that you haven't but should have covered.

Be mindful of potential leaders
While conducting the interviews, keep an eye out for individuals who display natural leadership qualities. Ask everyone open-ended questions like:

- Who do you think in the team has untapped potential?
- Is there anyone you admire in the company for their work ethic or ability to bring the team together?

- If you were to take on a leadership role, what would you change? (Only for people who you think could step up.)

These questions can reveal hidden talents and help you identify those who may be ready to step up. Sometimes your team will have a clearer perspective on who the real influencers are than you, especially if they work closely together.

Additionally, look for indirect indicators:

- **Outside interests:** If someone manages a side project, volunteers or has a hobby that requires organisation and leadership outside work, it could signal untapped potential.
- **Body language and enthusiasm:** Pay attention to when your team members light up during conversations. Those who get animated talking about certain projects or areas of the business are probably passionate and ready for more responsibility.

Post-interview follow-up

Once all interviews are complete, send a thank-you email to everyone involved. If suitable, share a brief overview of common themes and let them know their input will help shape the future of the company. Transparency is key — if team members see that their feedback is taken seriously and leads to improvements, they will be more inclined to share openly in the future.

Now you have gathered a wealth of insight, it's time to review and analyse the feedback. Prioritise the areas that need immediate attention and start making changes. Remember, doing nothing after asking for input is worse than not asking at all. According to AllVoices, only 38% of employees believe feedback will lead to change, while 18% are convinced it won't make any difference.[77] Prove them wrong by taking action. Consider whether a 'you said, we did' communication in the form of a poster or newsletter could be an option.

How to frame it for your team

You are about to share your vision for change with your team. This is a pivotal moment. The way you frame the changes you are about to make can either create excitement and buy-in or cause confusion and resistance. The truth is, nobody likes change for the sake of change, but when it's framed as progress — something that benefits everyone — your team is more likely to rally behind it. Here's how you can approach this conversation in a way that sets the right tone, builds trust and inspires confidence.

Own where you are
Start by acknowledging that things haven't always been perfect — and that's okay. This isn't about admitting defeat; it's about showing humility and a willingness to improve. Be open about the fact that some processes and structures or even your own leadership style might not have served the team as well as they could have. For example, you might say:

I've been reflecting on where we are as a company and where we want to go. I realise there are areas where we can improve – not just as a business but also in how I support and lead you as a team.'

By owning the current reality, you show your team that you're not just expecting them to change — you are committing to change too.

Share your vision
Paint a picture of the future you are working towards. What will the company look like when these changes are in place? How will

it feel to work there? Keep it simple, relatable and focused on the positive outcomes for everyone. For example:

'My goal is to create a workplace where we are all excited to come in every day, where everyone feels valued and supported and where we are all working towards the same vision. I want us to build a team culture that's not just productive but also enjoyable.'

Explain why
Help your team understand the reasoning behind the changes. Link it back to the goals of the business and the feedback you've gathered. This will help them see the bigger picture and understand that the changes are not arbitrary but strategic and meaningful. For example:

'We're making these changes because I believe we can do better – not just for our clients and the business but for each other. I've heard your feedback and it's clear that some things need to improve. These changes will help us work smarter and support each other better.'

Commit to changing yourself
This is where you will have to be a little bit vulnerable. Trust me, it will be worth the slight icky feeling you might be feeling right now reading this. As part of the process, you will need to explicitly state that you are committed to changing yourself as well. For example, you could phrase it something like this:

'I know I've made mistakes as a leader [and add something specific to you to make it meaningful: not being as available as you should have been, not giving enough feedback, being too controlling in some areas, changing your mind too often, etc.]. I want you to know that I am committed to working on those things. If I expect all of us to grow, I need to grow too.'

This vulnerability is key. It shows that you aren't just dictating change but leading by example.

Involve your team
Invite your team to be part of the process. This isn't just your journey — it's a collective effort. Ask for their input, ideas and support as you move forward. For example:

'This is not something I can do alone. I need your help to make these changes work. I want to hear your thoughts, ideas and feedback as we go through this process. Together, we can create something truly special.'

Set the tone for accountability
Finally, make it clear that this isn't just about words — it's about action. Let your team know that you are open to ongoing feedback and that you will hold yourself and others accountable for following through on the changes. For example:

'Change isn't always easy, but it is necessary. I'm asking all of us, including myself, to commit to this journey. If you see me falling back into old habits, I want you to call me out — just like I'll hold the team accountable to the standards we set together.'

In Chapter 4, you can find tips on how to ensure your team holds you accountable without feeling intimidated or worrying about their job.

BOSS facts – Part 3

#9: Trust is built, not demanded

'Trust' is the one word that was quoted most often in our company survey when we asked business owners what was most important to them about their teams. Trust is essential for any high-functioning team. Without it, you are left to double-check everything and micromanage everyone. But trust isn't a perk of your title — it's a privilege you must earn over time through actions and integrity. For a team to work effectively, they need to know you are dependable, transparent and consistent in how you lead.

It starts with small things: keeping your promises, being open about challenges and owning up to mistakes. It means showing your team you are willing to do what you ask of them and demonstrating you are invested in their success as much as your own. Trust requires vulnerability: share the 'why' behind your decisions and be honest about any uncertainties or limitations you may have. By opening up, you invite your team to do the same, and you create an environment where people feel safe to contribute ideas, take risks and admit when they need help. Trust is not built overnight, but by showing up consistently with respect and integrity, you will create a team that stands by you, even in the toughest of times.

#10: Feedback and trust are two-way streets

Feedback and trust might not be the same thing, but they share a crucial similarity: they both need to be able to flow in both directions. Too often, bosses assume that giving feedback is their job and receiving it is everyone else's. But here's the deal; if you aren't willing to listen and receive feedback yourself, you're missing out on one of the most powerful tools for growth and team engagement. According to a Salesforce survey, employees who feel their opinions are heard are 4.6 times more likely to feel empowered to do their best work.[28] When you're willing to listen to your team's input and act on it, you're not just gathering data or ticking a box, you are building trust and creating a culture — one where people feel safe to speak up, take risks and push boundaries.

When you ask for your team's perspective, you demonstrate that you don't see yourself as above them but that you're all in it together — working towards the same goals. Your team is much more likely to be honest with you if they see that you genuinely want to hear what they have to say — and if you actually act on their feedback. If you want your team to trust you, you will need to first trust them. The takeaway? Feedback without trust falls flat, and trust without feedback stalls progress. Encourage your team to share their thoughts and show them you are ready to hear them — even (or especially) if it's uncomfortable. When both feedback and trust truly go both ways, you create a culture that can produce magic.

#11: Listen more than you speak; it's the fastest way to learn

Ready for another truth bomb? If you do all the talking, you aren't learning anything new. The best leaders know listening isn't just a nice-to-have soft skill — it's a superpower. According to research by Zenger Folkman, leaders who are rated as great listeners are five times more likely to be seen as effective overall.[29] Why, you ask? Well, because when you listen, you gain insights, you uncover blind spots and you find opportunities that you would have otherwise missed.

Think about it: when was the last time you actually learned something while you were talking? Been a while, right? It is in those quiet moments — when you let go of the need for sharing your message, when you stop, listen and take in what is being said — that the real magic happens. Listening shows your team that you value their perspectives, which in turn — again — builds trust.

The bottom line is this: most people listen with the intent to reply, not to understand. Let's change that! Make it your mission to listen more than you speak, especially when your team is giving feedback, raising concerns or sharing ideas. Resist the urge to justify yourself or come up with all the reasons why their idea won't work. Listening isn't just the fastest way to learn, it's also the fastest way to earn respect.

#12: Don't watch the clock, watch the results

As the owner of the business, you might feel pressure to always be 'visible' to your team — whether that means working late, being the first in the office or staying online around the clock when working from home. Many bosses worry that if their team sees them leaving early or taking a break, they'll be perceived as slacking off or less committed. But here's the truth: it isn't about how long you are at your desk, it's about the impact you create.

When there is doubt about effectiveness — whether it's yours or your team's — it's easy to slip into 'clock-watching' mode. If your team doesn't trust your productivity, they may start monitoring the time you spend at work rather than focusing on results. Similarly, if you're unsure about your team's output, you may find yourself watching the hours they spend working instead of evaluating their performance. The cycle of mistrust and 'busy work' benefits no one and often leads to people waiting out the clock instead of producing meaningful results. What truly matters is the value you and your team create.

By prioritising results over time spent, you can create a culture of efficiency and trust. Demonstrate that great leadership isn't about long hours but about working smart, setting clear goals and empowering others to do the same. When your team sees you achieving big outcomes without being chained to your desk, they'll understand that productivity and wellbeing go hand in hand. So next time you feel the need to stay late just to 'set an example', ask yourself: am I focusing on the clock or the results? The best bosses lead by showing their team that it's the quality of the work — not the quantity of the hours — that drives success.

Claudia D **THOMPSON**

4. Strategise and Make It Happen

As you dive into this chapter, remember that change isn't a single event — it's an ongoing journey. Framing these changes effectively with your team is crucial, so if you need a refresher on communicating your vision, getting buy-in from your team and setting the tone for accountability, head back to Chapter 3. This chapter builds on everything you've learned so far, so it's important to keep the momentum going and ensure the team is on board with the direction you're heading.

By now you've probably uncovered a lot about yourself, your priorities and your team's unique dynamics. Maybe you've already seen subtle (or not so subtle) shifts — whether in your own mindset, your team's engagement or the overall vibe at work. That's fantastic! But don't stop now — this is where the real magic happens. In this chapter, we're pulling everything together. No more just thinking about it — it's time to turn insights into action and ideas into results. We'll start by locking in your all-star team, making sure you not only have the right people but that each person is in the role where they can shine, enjoy themselves and drive the business forward. From there, we'll dive into strategies that will take your vision off the page and turn it into reality. Let's get to work! Let's get started!

Getting everyone in position

First things first: before you can start planning the details of your new and improved organisational structure, you need to take a hard look at your team. Is everyone truly the right fit? Maybe there's someone who doesn't align with your values or lacks enthusiasm for what you're trying to build or whose negative attitude is dragging down the rest of the team.

You probably already have your own ideas about who might not be the best asset for the team, but sometimes personal feelings can cloud your judgement. A clear indicator that someone is not the right fit is if their name came up more than once during the interviews with your team members or if there have been recurring complaints from customers or suppliers. Bad behaviour, especially a negative attitude, should not be tolerated — even from high performers. Yes, they might hit their targets, but if they belittle colleagues or poison the team culture, they aren't worth the trouble. Tolerating their behaviour only demoralises the rest of the team, and all your efforts to get their input and buy-in become meaningless.

On the flip side, I've seen business owners let go of great people simply because they felt threatened by their skills or because their working style was different. Don't be that person! If someone is popular with the team, saves your company money by being more efficient, consistently delivers results and has an overall positive impact, they're probably not the problem. It's possible they're simply in the wrong seat (or they push one of your buttons — in which case it's worth taking a step back and asking yourself why. Are they challenging your perspective in ways that might actually benefit the team?).

Remember the question I mentioned previously: if you were hiring for the same role today, knowing what you now know about their skills and performance, would you hire them again? If the answer is 'not for their current role', then they're probably in the wrong position. If the answer is a firm 'no', then it's time to let them go. It might feel harsh, but hanging on to someone who doesn't fit or whom you don't see in the long-term vision for the business harms everyone — you, them and the rest of your team. As many business owners have told me, 'I should have fired people sooner' is often their biggest regret when reflecting on their past decisions.

Delaying the decision to part ways not only takes up your mental energy but also prevents the person from finding a role where they can find true fulfilment. As uncomfortable as it may be, letting go of people who are not the right fit is a definitive step towards creating a stronger, more motivated team. In some cases, temporarily reducing the team size is exactly what is needed to allow the rest of the team to regroup, dust off and move forward with renewed motivation and enthusiasm. Removing those who are harmful to team dynamics sends a powerful message to those who remain: *You are here for a reason. I appreciate you.*

Remember, each country has its own employment laws, so consult with an HR professional before taking any steps. On www.takecharge-thebook.com you can find a list of vetted HR consultancies to guide you through the process if you don't have an in-house HR team. A good HR professional will help you handle these transitions smoothly and in a way that's legally compliant.

Once you're sure you've got only the right people on the bus, it's time to take a look at your organisational structure to see if it's still fit for purpose. The goal here is to align your existing team with the ideal structure you created in Chapter 2. This is where you are matching your team's strengths and skills to the right roles — where you bridge the gap between your vision and reality. Start by revisiting the notes you made about your team members previously and the interview insights. You've already identified your team members' strengths, weaknesses, leadership potential and levels of engagement. Now it's time to use that information to position them in roles where they can truly excel.

Step 1: Assessing current roles and matching to the ideal structure

It's not just about placing people in positions and hoping for the best. It's about optimising their skills to drive your company forward. For instance, someone who has strong analytical abilities might never reach their full potential if they're stuck in a people-facing role. At the same time, someone who thrives on social interactions may feel stifled or underutilised in an analytical, behind-the-scenes position.

Start by reviewing the roles you are unsure about in your current setup and compare them with your ideal organisational chart. Are there gaps? Are there complete misfits? Is there anyone whose feedback (or the feedback from their colleagues) took you by surprise?

Sometimes a person was hired for one role but over time their position evolved and now no longer aligns with their strengths or the needs of the business. When creating new roles or redefining existing ones, focus on the natural strengths and weaknesses you have identified in each team member. This is not just about performance metrics or their current output but about finding where they can add the most value. For example, if someone excels at building strong team connections but struggles with strategic planning, it could be a better fit to place them in a role focused on managing people and get someone else to cover strategy. The key takeaway? Even the right person can do harm if they are in the wrong seat. A mismatch can lead to frustration, disengagement and even staff turnover, so make the time to get it right.

Step 2: Get an outsider's view

When rethinking and restructuring roles, it's so easy to fall into the trap of 'we have always done it this way'. To avoid this, consider bringing in an outsider's perspective — a coach, a consultant or even a fellow business owner. At the very least, do some research online for tips and best practices from other businesses. An unbiased perspective from someone who isn't personally invested can help you see beyond your present situation and objectively assess whether everything makes sense.

An outsider who is not too close to your business can review the ideal structure you created, compare it with the current setup and factor in your notes about the individual team members. Through the questions they'll ask — often just to understand why things were set up the way they are — they'll help you craft a setup that makes sense both strategically and practically. This can be invaluable, as we business owners are often too close to our teams and processes to make truly impartial decisions. Word of warning: when choosing your outsider, make sure it isn't someone who will just pay you lip service. You want someone who will challenge your thinking and offer honest feedback, not just agree with whatever you say. And, just as importantly, be open and flexible enough to actually listen to their advice and consider following it.

Step 3: Moving people to new roles with care

Once you've redesigned your structure, it's time to move people into the right seats. However, bear in mind the following key points:

Reward, don't punish: Changing someone's role should be a reward for high performance and engagement, not a reaction to unwanted behaviour. If someone is underperforming or showing behaviours that don't align with your culture, address those first. Remember, you can train someone in a skill, but you can't train attitude or cultural fit.

Win–win role changes: Role changes should be mutually beneficial. Don't move someone just because they demanded it or because you're worried they'll leave otherwise. If they aren't ready or don't show the right work ethic, it's better to wait. Be clear about the skills and behaviours they need to develop and support them with a plan if they're willing to put in the effort.

Role swapping and creative adjustments: Sometimes creating a new role from scratch doesn't make financial or organisational sense. Instead, have a look to see whether swapping roles between team members could be an option. Revisit your staff and interview notes to identify those who might be in the wrong positions. A strategic reshuffle could bring a fresh perspective to existing roles, leading to new ideas and more efficient approaches. But remember — communication is key. Do not decide over your team's head. Speak to the members individually to gauge their willingness and enthusiasm for a potential swap.

Step 4: Implementing the new structure and ongoing support

Once you've finalised your new structure on paper, it's time to put it into action.

Individual conversations: Before announcing any changes publicly, have one-on-one meetings with those whose roles are changing. Explain the reasons behind the shift, clarify their new responsibilities and set clear expectations. Ensure everyone understands not just the 'what' but also the 'why' behind their new position. Allow plenty of time for their questions.

Training and development plans: A new role is rarely an instant fit. Provide ongoing training, coaching and support. Just because someone is willing, it doesn't mean they're fully prepared. For individuals stepping into leadership roles, training is particularly critical. Effective leaders need tools, frameworks and confidence to guide their teams and deliver results. Consider bringing in external training providers to support this development. They can introduce specialised skills and offer an outsider's perspective that may not be obvious from within your organisation. Investing in external training is not just an expense — it's a strategic move that equips your team with the knowledge and tools to succeed in the long term.

Monitor and adjust: After the reshuffle, keep a close eye on how the new structure is impacting productivity, morale and business results. Collect regular feedback from your team on what is working and what needs a bit more adjusting. Remember, an organisational structure shouldn't be static — it evolves as the company (and the people in it) grows. Encourage your team to stay adaptable and open to change, making it clear that adjustments can and will be made as needed.

Making the rules for the team

Up to this point, it has been just you, working in isolation, making decisions about *your* idea for a perfect business. Now it's time to change perspective and involve the players that can help bring that business to life. Over the following pages we will be defining your company's mission, vision, the core values you want your business to exude and the rules of the game that your team is playing.

For that, you will need to schedule a series of group workshops to bring everyone together. Workshops might sound daunting if you've never run one before, but don't worry too much. This is simply about getting your team in a room and having a structured conversation. You don't need to be a professional facilitator; you just need to create the space where people can come together, ideas can flow and decisions get made. A brainstorming session is most productive with around 5 to 8 participants — enough to capture a variety of perspectives without the conversation becoming overwhelming or unfocused. Depending on your team size, this might mean starting with a smaller core group rather than involving the entire team right away. However, if your business is small, it's perfectly fine to include the whole team from the start.

If you do start with a core group, avoid the risk of ending up with the same voices and dynamics that might have shaped the status quo, just repackaged with a new label. To do this, make a deliberate effort to include team members you haven't consulted before — those who bring fresh perspectives you identified in earlier chapters. Their influence will be critical in getting buy-in from the rest of the team.

Once the group has crafted initial ideas for your company's purpose, values and rules, present these outcomes in a full-team General Assembly. Use this broader meeting to gather feedback, refine the ideas and ensure every team member feels included, heard and aligned with the company's new direction. This two-step approach not only keeps the discussions manageable but also creates a sense of ownership and commitment across the team. So go ahead, pick your core team or gather everyone if that makes sense for your business. If you're bringing in the whole team from the start, keep reading through to page 150 before hosting any workshops — there you'll find extra tips for running an all-team assembly effectively.

For now, let's turn your focus to crafting your company's higher purpose.

Defining your company's purpose: Setting the course for your team

After you've found the right seat for everyone and everyone is happy and beginning to settle in, it's time to decide where your business is headed next. To stick with the bus analogy, you are now putting it to a vote where the journey is going. While you, as the driver, will ultimately have the final say, the passengers get to give their input to ensure they are fully on board. If your team isn't happy with the destination, don't be surprised if they jump off at the next stop. The reality is, if they don't believe in (or simply don't realise) where the bus is going, they might catch a ride on a different one instead.

You might be wondering, 'why bother with a purpose statement when we've been getting along just fine without one?' Well, here's the thing: businesses that operate with a higher purpose consistently outperform those that only focus on the bottom line. Investors, customers and employees alike are increasingly looking beyond just the financials. Today, a clear purpose is no longer just a nice-to-have but a must if you want to retain great talent and attract even more in the future. When your team believes in the company's purpose, they are more likely to innovate, go above and beyond and find solutions that benefit not just the business but the wider community as well.

According to the *Harvard Business Review*, a staggering 70% of people can't recite their company's strategy or purpose.[30] This usually means one of three things: they don't know it, they don't understand it or they feel so disconnected from it that it doesn't influence their day-to-day work. In these cases, the purpose becomes practically useless. I remember sitting in an all-team meeting where the boss proudly declared, 'We all know our company's goals and we can all do our part to meet them.' Cue awkward silence and nervous glances. Misreading the room, the boss singled out a staff member and asked him to remind everyone what the goal was. The poor guy, caught off guard, admitted he didn't know. A few hesitant nods from others confirmed it wasn't just him. Thankfully, before turning it into a quiz show, the boss took a step back and clarified the goal — something many team members confessed afterwards was the first time they had ever heard it.

For a purpose statement to be effective, it needs to be known by every member of your team. It should be simple, concise and easy to recite. Don't try to be too clever — complexity only leads to confusion. The best statements are those that can be clearly understood and remembered, even under pressure. A purpose statement outlines your company's long-term aspirations, focusing on the impact you want to make on the world. Simply put, it defines where you are headed, what you do and why you do it. Sometimes the terms 'vision', 'mission' and 'purpose' are used interchangeably, and many companies opt to call it something else entirely, like a 'purpose statement' or 'why we do what we do' section on their website. If these terms don't resonate with you, feel free to choose something that does. What is crucial is not the label but the content. The substance of your purpose is far more important than the terminology you use.

A company's purpose is typically set by the owner or the leadership team. It defines where you are going and what you're trying to build. But here's the catch: a powerful purpose shouldn't be confined to you and your leadership circle. It needs to be the north star that guides every single person in your organisation. It helps each team member understand the role they play in the bigger picture and can ignite motivation to push beyond the status quo.

You might have heard the story of President Kennedy's visit to the NASA Space Centre in 1962. During his visit, he noticed a janitor carrying a broom and went over to introduce himself. 'What are you doing?' Kennedy asked. The janitor replied proudly, 'I am helping put a man on the moon, Mr President.' That janitor understood the importance of his contribution; he knew he was a valuable part of something far bigger than himself. He wasn't merely a cleaner — he was a member of the 1962 NASA Space Mission. *That* is the level of pride and confidence you want to instil in your team. That is the goal: to create a purpose so compelling that every team member, no matter their role, feels they are part of something bigger.

A good purpose statement (or whatever you call it) typically includes three parts:

1. **What you do:** The core product or services you offer.
2. **How you do it:** The unique processes or approaches you use.
3. **Why you do it:** The deeper reason behind your business beyond profit.

A well-crafted purpose statement can transform your team's engagement and drive. It becomes the foundation for decision making, goal setting and everyday actions. So, as you embark on this next phase, remember that defining where you are headed is just as important as ensuring you've got the right people in the right seats.

Workshop: Defining your company's mission

While this exercise outlines one possible process to create a purpose statement, it's important to remember that coming up with a statement that can stand solidly for decades is no small feat. If you get stuck, it might make sense to hire a professional brand strategist for guidance.

For your purpose statement to truly resonate, the vision outlined in it needs to reflect the entire company's aspirations. If your team thinks your vision is too lofty or disconnected from their interests, it won't be effective. For your first brainstorming and thought-gathering session choose a setting that encourages creativity and collaboration — ideally away from the usual distractions of the office. Before diving in, clearly explain the purpose of the session: to articulate a compelling and authentic purpose that will unify and motivate the entire team. Allow enough time for an open, focused discussion and remind your team that this is an important step towards shaping the company's future together.

Start with your company's foundations

The best place to start is at the beginning. Your purpose statement should answer the big-picture questions about your company. Start by brainstorming the following questions with the group:

- What is the business's main purpose?
- Why does what you do matter? Why do you do it?
- What difference do you want to make in your industry or community?
- What does success look like beyond profit?
- How do you want to impact society or the environment?

- If your company achieved everything it set out to do, how would the world be different? When would you know you've 'made it'?
- How do you want to make a difference to society and the wider community?
- What does your company offer your customers? Why do you exist?
- Who does your company serve? Who is your target customer?
- Why does your company stand out? What makes you different from your competitors?

At this stage, also revisit the business goals you set in Chapter 2. Discuss how these goals align with your vision for a better world. What might success look like beyond profit? Could it mean market expansion, developing new products or becoming a leader in your industry? What accolades would you want to receive?

While working through these questions, start noting keywords and attributes that come up. Don't judge or filter the words yet — just write them down. You may need these when simplifying your statement later.

Sort your answers

After this initial brainstorming phase, you should have plenty of material. Well done! Now put all of it aside for a few days. This allows your subconscious to mull it over so you can come back to it with fresh eyes. When you're ready, gather your vision team again and review everything you've written down, plus add any additional thoughts that came up during the few days off. With a highlighter, mark the ideas and phrases that resonate the most with the group. Sort these by importance. Don't disregard the non-highlighted ideas — they could still be useful for defining core values, a company roadmap or even your business plan.

Draft your statement

Now you've narrowed down your key phrases, it's time to draft your purpose statement. Start organising the most important concepts into sentences that flow well. At this stage, don't worry too much about length. Focus on making it comprehensive, covering all key points and ensuring it feels authentic. It's possible that during this process your team might come up with a few different versions of the statement. That's perfectly normal. The goal here is to explore different ways of expressing your company's vision and mission, so don't be afraid to experiment. Unless you're a unicorn (which you might well be!), your first draft probably won't be the final version. Once you've drafted one or more versions, let them sit for a few days to allow everyone time to reflect. During this review phase, ask yourself and your team:

- Is it ambitious enough? Is it too ambitious?
- Does it accurately reflect your company?
- Does it make sense? (Share it with family members to ensure it's understandable from an outside perspective and consider their comments.)

After a few days, revisit the drafts and refine them. Take out any unnecessary bits, rephrase sections and use synonyms to simplify where possible. This back-and-forth process with your team is crucial — don't rush it.

Examples for inspiration

Sometimes looking at examples can help spark ideas when you're stuck. Here are a few powerful purpose statements from well-known companies.

Patagonia: To protect our home planet.

Microsoft: To empower every person and every organization on the planet to achieve more.

Nike: To bring inspiration and innovation to every athlete in the world (if you have a body, you are an athlete).

Google: To organize the world's information and make it universally accessible and useful.

Unilever: To make sustainable living commonplace.

Airbnb: To create a world where anyone can belong anywhere.

Starbucks: To inspire and nurture the human spirit — one person, one cup, and one neighborhood at a time.

See how these statements paint an inspiring picture of the future while leaving room for individual interpretation? Every employee can see how their daily work contributes to the broader mission. Now you've defined your purpose and values, it's time to look at your core values — the attributes you want your company to portray to both the outside and your team.

Crafting your core values

Almost as a byproduct of the purpose exercise, you may have already identified some values that naturally align with your company's ethos. In this section, we will focus on solidifying those values to serve as the foundation of your business. These will help guide hiring decisions, product development and even selecting the right suppliers. Your core values shouldn't just be a list of generic words like *honesty, integrity* or *positivity*. Instead, they should be authentic principles that reflect how you and your team truly operate on a daily basis. These values can even take the form of short actionable phrases that everyone in the business is happy to live and work by.

I once worked with a company that proudly declared they had 14 core values. The result? The values were close to meaningless: some people lived by values 2, 3 and 7, others by 1, 5 and 8, while still others preferred values 10, 11 and 14. The truth is, 14 core values are far too many. To be effective, values must be clear, memorable and actionable. Aim for four to six core values to capture the essence of your business. This focus will ensure your values are easy to remember and actually influence day-to-day decisions and behaviours.

Workshop: Defining your core values

To identify the values that will guide your business, gather your core team for another brainstorming session and follow the following steps.

Start with inspiration

Ask each team member to think about their favourite colleague and write down the top five values that person consistently demonstrates. This will reveal the real, lived values within your organisation.

Envision the ideal team

Next, ask everyone to list the values they would love to see in their fellow team members. This provides insight into what your team truly values in their work environment and colleagues.

Tip: Let the whole team participate in steps 1 and 2 by inviting them to submit their top five attributes by email or anonymously via an ideas box in the office.

Collect and refine

Have the team members write down at least five values they think are most important on sticky notes. Collect them all on a wall. Then identify trends. Which words appear most frequently? Can some ideas be grouped together? Compile all the attributes on a whiteboard or flipchart — no judgement, just brainstorming. Then review each attribute and cross off those that feel less essential. Repeat this process until you are left with a handful of values that you want to reflect your company's ethos.

Establishing the rules of the game

Until this point, you might have been working with just a small group to draft your vision, mission and core values. Now it's time to open it up to everyone if you haven't already. This is where you need to call an all-staff meeting and get the whole team involved. It's time to *call in the troops* (insert fanfare sound here). Oh yes, you heard me! It's time for the General Assembly. You are getting everyone together — from the newest temp to the longest-serving employee, from the ones who are always up for a meeting to the ones who would rather sit through a tax audit than another team discussion. This is where you reveal everything you've been working on for the past few weeks.

Why bother with an all-staff meeting? Because if you want your team to be cohesive, team members need to see and hear each other regularly. In businesses with different departments or split locations (like office staff and warehouse teams), people might otherwise rarely mingle. A quarterly General Assembly can help bridge that gap.

But why stop there? Why not give this gathering a unique name that relates to your business and makes it feel more personal? Get creative and involve the team in choosing the name — something that creates a sense of belonging. Think 'the Collins Convention' (if your business name is Collins), 'the Parsons Parley' for a business called Parsons or 'the Hartford Huddle' for the Hartford Group — you get the picture. The point is to let your team make it their own to increase their buy-in.

No matter what you call it, this meeting is your chance to discuss the exciting progress you've made and get everyone's input on the next steps. For this first session — where you will be brainstorming, collecting and summarising ideas — it might be helpful to have an external facilitator. A facilitator ensures topics keep moving, the session stays on track and everyone gets a chance to speak.

Before the meeting:
- Send out an agenda ahead of time. Clearly outline the meeting's objectives and emphasise that everyone's input is essential for shaping the company's future.
- Break the session into clear parts: purpose, values and rules of the game. This helps everyone know where to focus their thoughts.
- Set time limits for each discussion topic and designate someone to take notes. Choose your facilitation tools: whiteboard, flipchart or digital tools.
- Encourage everyone to come prepared with ideas.

During the meeting:
- Create a safe and open environment. Start with a quick icebreaker to get everyone comfortable. Establish that the meeting is a judgement-free zone and nobody has anything to worry about.
- Before opening the floor for each exercise, get everyone to jot down their thoughts. This will particularly encourage your quieter team members to participate and ensures more thoughtful contributions.
- Use round-robin brainstorming. Go around the room, allowing each person to share one idea at a time. This prevents more dominant voices from taking over.
- If your team is large, consider splitting into smaller groups for discussions before coming back together and getting a spokesperson from each group to present their ideas.
- Encourage people to work with someone they don't usually interact with. It's a great way to build cross-departmental relationships.
- If you notice that certain individuals haven't contributed, invite them warmly (and without too much pressure) to share their thoughts.
- Invite everyone to share additional thoughts after the meeting with you in writing.

Part 1: Your purpose statement

This is where you gather feedback on the purpose statements you drafted earlier. To get meaningful feedback, consider asking questions like:

- Which of these statements do you like the most and why?
- Which of these statements do you like the least and why?
- Is there anything you think is missing?
- Do you have any other ideas?

Part 2: Your core values

Now it's time to get your team's input on the values put together by your core team. To ensure the values truly resonate with everyone across the organisation, involve the whole team in refining them. Present the team with the (up to) 10 values that came up most often and then consider asking the following questions:

- Which of these values do you connect with the most? And why?
- Are there any values that don't resonate or that feel out of place? If so, why?
- Do you feel there is a value that is missing? If so, what would you add?
- How would you define these values in your own words?

For both, encourage team members to be candid with their feedback. This is their chance to shape the company's culture and to make the purpose statement and the values more than just words on paper but principles that guide daily actions and decisions.

Part 3: The rules of the game

This part will probably take up the most time in your meeting, so, depending on how much time you've already spent on the first two parts, consider scheduling a follow-up session if needed, because now it's time to define the rules that will guide how your team operates. To kick things off, use the sports team analogy: just as in any sport, clear rules are essential for smooth play.

Workshop: Setting the rules of the game

Start by sharing your 'boss rules', which you crafted in Chapter 2. Explain that these are the rules that you, as the boss, are responsible for setting because they impact the business's integrity, legal standing and overall mission. Once those non-negotiables are established, it's time for your team to create the rest of the 'rules of the game'. These rules can be more flexible and are designed to enhance teamwork, communication and the overall work environment. By giving your team a voice in creating these rules, you empower them to take ownership and accountability. When everyone participates in crafting the playbook, they are more likely to uphold it. Here are some of the topics to cover during this process.

Meeting etiquette

These rules set expectations for how meetings are run to ensure they are efficient and respectful of everyone's time.

Questions to consider:
- How often should meetings be scheduled? How long should they last?
- What are the expectations for arriving on time and being prepared?
- Are phones and laptops allowed during meetings? Or should they be put away to maintain focus?
- Should someone be assigned to take minutes and distribute them afterwards?

Communication guidelines

These rules determine how your team communicates, both internally and externally, to maintain clear and effective channels.

Questions to consider:
- What communication channels should be used for different types of messages (e.g. for quick chats, for formal communication)?
- What are the expected response times?
- How should urgent issues be communicated? What defines an 'urgent' issue?
- How do we ensure communication remains respectful, clear and constructive?
- How do we keep each other informed about progress?

Collaboration and support

These rules help your team work together effectively and support one another in achieving shared goals.

Questions to consider:
- How can team members best share knowledge and resources across departments?
- What are the expectations for offering help when someone is struggling or needs support?
- How should project ownership be managed to avoid misunderstandings?
- How do we ensure all relevant people are involved?
- How can we encourage cross-departmental collaboration without stepping on each other's toes?

Conflict resolution

These rules outline how your team handles disagreements and resolves conflicts to maintain a healthy work environment.

Questions to consider:
- What is the preferred approach for addressing conflicts — one-on-one conversations, mediated discussions, group meetings?
- What steps should team members take if they feel uncomfortable addressing a conflict directly?
- How can we ensure conflicts are resolved constructively and without blame?
- How can we create a safe space for open dialogue and honest feedback?

Celebrating wins

These rules define how your team acknowledges successes, big or small, to maintain morale and a positive culture.

Questions to consider:
- How often should we celebrate team achievements (weekly, monthly, quarterly, as they happen)?
- What types of achievements are worth celebrating (project completions, personal milestones, birthdays)?
- How do we ensure celebrations are inclusive and meaningful for everyone?
- Who decides when and how we celebrate? How can team members contribute ideas?

Shared spaces etiquette

These rules ensure communal areas are respected and maintained for everyone's comfort.

Questions to consider:
- What are the guidelines for keeping common areas (e.g. kitchens, meeting rooms) tidy?

- How should people handle shared resources, such as printers, office supplies and equipment?
- Are there any rules around eating in shared spaces (I am looking at you, smelly fish lunch!)?
- How can we encourage everyone to take responsibility for maintaining a clean and welcoming workspace?

Throughout the process, let your team do most of the talking. Unless their suggestions are entirely unreasonable, give their ideas a chance. Remember, all changes come with a probationary period. If something isn't working, you can adjust it later, but resist the urge to backtrack to old ways just because 'we've always done it like that'. These new rules crafted together are your team's commitment to a more purposeful and harmonious workplace.

After the meeting, share the notes and send out a summary of the session with key takeaways, decisions made and the next steps.

The code word

One of the most challenging aspects of introducing and encouraging accountability in a team is empowering people to speak up — especially when it comes to addressing the boss. Let's face it: calling out your boss can feel intimidating, even in the most open environment. To make this easier, we are going to create a team-specific 'code word' that acts as a neutral, positive and fun reminder for everyone to stay on track with the changes you are working towards. Here's how it works:

Explain the purpose
Start by letting your team know that this exercise is about creating a safe and light-hearted way to keep each other accountable. Frame it as a tool that everyone can use — not just to remind you, the boss, but to keep each other aligned with the team's new rules and goals.

Brainstorm together
Ask the team to come up with a word or phrase that feels positive, neutral and perhaps a little quirky to keep things light-hearted. It could be something completely random like 'pineapple', 'unicorn' or, my personal favourite, 'cheese'! The key is that it should be memorable and inject a little humour into the moment.

Agree on the rules
Once you've chosen a word, set clear guidelines for its use. For example:

- The code word can be used in any meeting, discussion or situation where someone feels the team (or an individual) is slipping back into old habits.
- It is not a judgement — it's a friendly reminder that brings everyone back to the bigger picture.
- The code word should be used sparingly to maintain its impact and avoid overuse.

Practise together
Do a quick role-play scenario as a team where someone uses the word in a non-threatening way. This helps everyone feel more comfortable and normalises its use in the workplace.

Commit to using it

End the exercise by committing as a team to using the code word whenever it's needed. Reassure your team that this is a tool for growth, not criticism, and that it's okay to make mistakes as you all learn to work in new ways. As the boss, it's especially important to emphasise that using the code word against you is a safe space. Let your team know that there will be no negative repercussions for calling you out and, in fact, you welcome it as a way to help everyone — including yourself — stay accountable.

Alternative ideas to reduce intimidation

If you feel the code word exercise might not resonate with your team, here are a few other approaches to make accountability less scary.

- **Anonymous feedback channels**: Set up an anonymous online form or suggestion box where team members can share feedback about what's working and what is not.
- **Buddy system**: Pair each team member with someone they can check in with regularly and who can gently call them out when needed. However, be mindful when assigning pairs — avoid matching people who already tend to form cliques together. The goal is to encourage constructive accountability and foster connections across the team, not to reinforce existing group dynamics or exclusionary behaviour.
- **Regular check-ins**: Commit to regular team retrospectives where everyone (including you) reflects on what is working and areas for improvement. This normalises feedback as a team-wide practice rather than an individual confrontation.

Bringing the theory to life

Once your team has defined the company's purpose and core values and agreed the rules of the game, don't let them gather dust on a poster or in a handbook. Instead, integrate them into every aspect of your business. Start by adding them to your website. Explain not just what they are but why they matter and how they will guide the decisions and behaviour of the company. From there, make these principles a consistent part of everyday work life. Reference them during team meetings, include them in your employee policies (a good HR consultant can help with that), use them to frame decisions and weave them into your recognition and reward systems. For example, if one of your values is 'collaboration', highlight examples of teamwork during meetings or recognise individuals who go above and beyond to help their colleagues. By making your vision and values actionable and visible, you ensure that they stay top of mind and become part of your company's DNA.

Remember, your purpose and values are not set in stone. While they should guide your business for years to come, they can evolve as your company grows and changes. However, avoid changing them too frequently, as this can dilute their impact.

Making the rules for the individual

Welcome to the section affectionately nicknamed 'the acronym section'. You will soon see why — and you might even wonder where all the plain, old-fashioned titles have gone. Don't worry; we'll make sense of it all. By now, you and your team have a powerful vision. You know where you are going, why it matters and how to get there. The pieces are coming together beautifully. But the question remains: how do you ensure the results you have created in the previous chapters last for the long haul? This section is all about making those results stick — turning your vision, rules and culture into everyday actions. It's now time to assign ownership, measure progress, celebrate wins and continuously engage your team.

Numbers play a big part in that. They are an essential tool for maintaining clarity and accountability. That's why we are now giving everyone a number. No, we aren't numbering your employees, but we'll assign measurable outcomes to help everyone understand what is expected of them and make it easy to track progress. Numbers cut through the noise of ambiguity and create accountability, clarity and a sense of ownership. They can also motivate your team to strive for improvement while promoting healthy competition and teamwork. However, numbers are only as effective as the framework and the thought process behind them. Not every goal-setting method will be a perfect fit for every business, and that's okay. Take note of what's out there, see what resonates with you and don't be afraid to mix, adapt or even create your own approach. Let's look at some common accountability systems and how to choose one that best fits your business:

KPIs (Key Performance Indicators)
KPIs are specific, measurable targets — think sales numbers, customer satisfaction scores or project completion rates. While they provide clarity and structure, they can become problematic if they are too rigid, unrealistic or irrelevant to your team's personal motivations.

OKRs (Objectives and Key Results)
- OKRs shift the focus to broader objectives and the measurable results that indicate progress toward those objectives. For example:
    - Objective: Increase customer satisfaction by 25%
    - Key results: Achieve a 4.7 average feedback score and retain 85% of clients annually
- OKRs are collaborative and adaptable, but they can feel overwhelming in fast-changing environments.

SMART goals
Specific, Measurable, Achievable, Relevant, Time-bound — a classic framework that works well for small, actionable objectives but may feel restrictive for larger, more flexible goals.

BHAGs (Big Hairy Audacious Goals)
A concept first mentioned by Jim Collins in *Built to Last*, these are the 'let's aim for the moon' kind of goals meant to inspire and unite your team under one bold vision. BHAGs align with your company's mission and stretch the boundaries of what seems possible. They are aspirational, not operational, and should complement rather than replace smaller, measurable goals. (Think: we are going to put a man on the moon before this decade is out and return him safely to Earth.)

CFR (Conversations, Feedback, Recognition)
A framework focused on ongoing dialogue and performance tracking rather than fixed outcomes. Perfect for staying adaptable while keeping engagement high.

NCT (Narrative, Commitments, Tasks)
A flexible alternative to OKRs that breaks the goals into a compelling narrative, measurable commitments and actionable tasks. This method works particularly well in dynamic, fast-moving environments.

OGSM (Objective, Goals, Strategies, Measures)
A more detailed framework that aligns overarching business objectives with specific strategies and measurable milestones.

MBO (Management by Objectives)
MBO aligns individual and team goals with company-wide objectives. This approach is particularly suited for collaboration between managers and employees to set, track and evaluate performance.

With so many frameworks to choose from, it's easy to feel overwhelmed. But here's the good news: you don't have to get it perfect on your first try. The most important thing is to start somewhere. Pick a framework that feels like the best fit for your business right now and see how it goes. If it doesn't work out as planned, you can adjust or refine it or even create your own hybrid approach tailored to your unique team and goals. When deciding on a framework, consider the following tips:

- **Simplicity first**: If you're just starting out, opt for a straightforward system like SMART goals or KPIs. You can always add complexity later.
- **Team dynamics**: Think about your team's working style. Are they big-picture thinkers who thrive on ambitious goals like BHAGs or do they prefer the clarity of more specific targets like OKRs?
- **Business stage**: Early-stage startups may need more flexibility (NCT or CFR), while established businesses can benefit from structured systems like OGSM and MBO.
- **Industry and culture**: Align the framework with your company's mission and values. For example, innovation-driven teams might prefer frameworks that inspire creativity, while data-focused teams may lean toward measurable KPIs.

Knowing what to measure: Clarity and ownership

For your team to perform at its best, everyone needs to be crystal clear on what is expected of them. Without clarity, it is impossible for anyone to excel, let alone work independently (to free up your time). Setting measurable, role-specific goals ensures your team members understand their responsibilities, stay motivated and contribute to the larger vision.

One of the most effective ways to establish clarity is through positional contracts. A positional contract is a document that acts as the ultimate guide for each team member. Think of it as their personal playbook. It outlines not only what is expected from them but also how they can excel in their role. And if you ever need to rehire for the position, having this document in place will make the process a lot easier — not only by giving you a clear picture of what to look for in a new hire but also by setting expectations right from the interview stage.

Exercise: Creating positional contracts

For the first draft, ask the person currently holding the position to write their own version of the positional contract. This exercise helps you understand how *they* perceive their role and provides a foundation for further discussion if needed. Once the draft is complete, sit down together to refine it. Discuss the specific expectations and goals of the role in detail. The final document should be something you both feel proud of — clear, actionable and aligned with the company's mission.

What to include in a positional contract:

- **Role summary**: A concise description of the position's purpose and how it contributes to the overall business objectives.
- **Core responsibilities**: The primary tasks the role entails, broken down into actionable points.
- **Measurable goals**: Specific numbers tied to the post-holder's responsibilities.
- **Decision-making authority**: Clarity on what decisions the individual can make independently vs when they need approval.

> - **Reporting expectations**: Who do they report to? How? How often should they update them on their progress?
> - **Team interaction and collaboration**: Expectations for working with colleagues, working on cross-departmental projects or mentoring others.

Positional contracts are more than just paperwork — they are the backbone of a high-functioning team. When combined with meaningful goals and regular check-ins, they provide the structure your team needs to flourish within clear and consistent boundaries.

Not all roles lend themselves to obvious performance metrics. You might be wondering how to know what to measure or what numbers to assign people. While sales and marketing roles often have clear targets like revenue or customer acquisition, others, such as IT or HR, require a bit more creativity. Here are some examples:

Executive Assistant:
- Ensure 100% accuracy in scheduling.
- Complete 95% of tasks within agreed deadlines.
- Respond to 90% of emails within one business day.

Customer Service Representative:
- Resolve 80% of issues within 24 hours.
- Achieve a 4.5/5 customer satisfaction score.

IT Support:
- Maintain system uptime of 99.5%.
- Resolve 90% of tickets within 24 hours.

HR Manager:
- Ensure 100% compliance with all employment laws and regulations by conducting quarterly audits and updating company policies as needed.

- Reduce new hire onboarding time by 20% while maintaining a 90% satisfaction rate among new hires in onboarding surveys.

The key for every role is to connect daily tasks to measurable outcomes. Be specific, relevant and realistic when setting these goals.

Additional tips for effective goal setting

- **Spread goals equally**: Avoid overloading your high performers while giving token goals to others. Aim for a fair distribution of responsibilities.
- **Focus on activities**: Instead of fixating only on outcomes, track the activities that lead to success (e.g. calls made rather than deals closed).
- **Keep goals fresh**: Revisit and adjust goals quarterly to ensure they remain relevant and motivational and to spot any issues early on.
- **Balance performance**: Remember, goals are just one part of the picture. A team member's attitude, teamwork and engagement are equally important.

By clearly defining what to measure, creating positional contracts and aligning goals with individual motivators, you are setting the foundation for a team that's both autonomous and high performing. It's not about micromanaging; it's about creating clarity, accountability and empowerment. With these systems in place, your team will have the direction it needs to succeed and the independence to make it happen.

Remember, the perfect framework is the one that works for your team, fits your goals and gets results. Don't feel like you have to assign everyone a perfectly defined goal straight away. Instead, focus on giving each team member a number or value they can aim towards — a benchmark for success that aligns with their role and contributes to the bigger picture. It doesn't have to be as descriptive or formal as KPIs, but there must be some way to measure everyone's contribution.

If you're unsure what to measure, put it up for discussion with the individual themselves. You might be surprised by the ideas they come up with, as they probably have valuable insights into what success in their role looks like. By involving them in the process, not only do you get actionable suggestions but you also increase their buy-in and engagement with the goals set for them. Remember, the goal isn't to overcomplicate things — it's to provide clarity and focus.

Maintaining momentum

You've done the hard work of building a vision, setting clear goals and defining the rules of the game — you've created the foundation for a great team culture. Now comes the hardest and most rewarding part: keeping the momentum alive for the long haul. Sustaining momentum needs more than just hitting numbers — it's about embedding habits, maintaining motivation and keeping your team engaged and aligned with your mission. So, let's look at some strategies to make your team's success a long-term reality.

Reflect, reset and repeat

Reflection isn't just a look back; it's a powerful tool for looking forward. Regularly taking time to evaluate progress, celebrate wins and refine strategies helps keep your team moving in the right direction. And the single most important way to maintain momentum? Regular check-ins with your team. There is absolutely no way around them. They are usually the first thing to get dropped when things get busy — but ironically, that's when they matter most. If you want to keep people engaged, aligned and accountable, you'll need to make these meetings a non-negotiable part of your routine. Here's how to incorporate reflection and resets into your leadership playbook.

Review goals quarterly

Progress happens when goals are relevant, realistic and inspiring. As the business evolves, so should your targets. Use quarterly reviews to revisit team and individual goals. Have an open discussion with your team: what is working? What isn't? Are there external factors that have impacted progress? Adjust the goals as necessary to keep them fresh, achievable and aligned with your company's vision. Resetting goals when needed isn't a sign of failure — it's a way to keep your team's focus on what matters.

Team reflection sessions

Dedicate time to structured team reflection sessions. These meetings allow your team to pause, share insights and realign. Ask questions like:

- What were our biggest wins this past quarter?
- What challenges did we face? How did we overcome them?
- What lessons can we take forward?

Make these sessions fun and engaging by incorporating team-building activities or celebrating progress with snacks, awards or shoutouts. This reinforces the importance of reflection while maintaining a positive and forward-thinking atmosphere.

Encourage individual self-reflection

Personal accountability begins with self-awareness. Encourage your team members to regularly evaluate their own contributions. Provide simple prompts to guide their reflection, such as:

- What have I achieved this month? What am I proud of?
- Where can I improve? What support do I need?
- How am I contributing to the team's success and our shared mission?

Self-reflection not only aids personal growth but also helps individuals feel more connected to their roles and the broader company vision.

Embed reflection into your culture

Reflection isn't just a periodic activity — it's a habit that should be ingrained in your culture. Here is how to make it part of your team's DNA:

- **Start meetings with a win:** Begin every meeting by asking team members to share one small win they had recently. It sets a positive tone and reinforces the idea that progress, no matter how small, is worth celebrating.
- **Create a feedback-driven culture:** Feedback isn't just for check-ins; it's a continuous loop. Celebrate what is going well and address areas of improvement in real time. Teach your team to view feedback as a tool for growth, not criticism.
- **Encourage micro-resets:** Encourage your team to view every setback as an opportunity for a micro-reset. Whether it's a missed deadline or a tough customer interaction, help them see that every challenge is a chance to reassess, recalibrate and come back stronger.

The power of recognition and feedback

Numbers and goals are great tools to have. They provide crucial structure to the business, but it is actually recognition and feedback that breathe life into your workplace culture. A team that feels appreciated, seen and supported will happily go the extra mile.

Celebrate successes: Celebrating wins is one of the simplest ways to keep morale high and reinforce behaviours (plus it's a great way to liven up an otherwise same old, same old working day). Whether it is hitting a major milestone or a small achievement, find ways to acknowledge effort and progress. This could range from a heartfelt thank-you during a team meeting to a formal reward for reaching quarterly goals. Recognition is not just about grand gestures — simply showing you've noticed a positive behaviour you want to see more of can make a big difference.

Praise in public, criticise in private: Public recognition can do wonders for the mood in the office and inspires others to do better too. After all, everybody loves being recognised for their hard work from time to time. On the other hand, nobody likes being told off or criticised in public. It is not only terrible for the individual but also makes the other members of your team nervous, wondering if they could be next. Constructive criticism is best delivered in private and with empathy. When addressing areas of improvement, focus on behaviours rather than personal traits, and always provide actionable steps for improvement (see BOSS fact #4: Keep it FAB).

Fuel long-lasting success with alignment and action

Momentum doesn't die out because people stop caring - it dies when they stop seeing progress. If you want long-term success, you need two things: alignment and action. Your team needs to feel like they're moving forward with purpose and not just spinning their wheels. Here's how to stay in motion:

Tie performance to purpose: Make it impossible for your team to feel like their work is 'just a job'. During check-ins or team meetings, regularly connect their individual achievements to your company's mission and values. Let your team know their daily actions contribute to something bigger than themselves.

Let them drive: Momentum develops when people feel in control. Give your team ownership over their goals and instead of micromanaging, act as their coach: celebrate their success and provide guidance when needed. When they own their progress, they'll be more invested and willing to contribute.

Keep it fresh: When things get stale or go back to the old ways, momentum stalls. Regularly invite your team to challenge the status quo: What's working? What's not? What ideas do they have for improving processes? Creating space for innovation keeps things fresh and exciting.

Lead by example – always

As the boss, whatever you do sets the tone for your team. If you want your team to stay motivated, engaged and aligned with the new direction of the business, you need to demonstrate those behaviours yourself. Show up with energy, embrace the vision you created and live by the rules that you've agreed with the team. Hold your team accountable to their goals, be positive, and stay open to innovation and learning new things, and guess what? Your team will naturally follow suit. They will see that going back to the old ways is not an option and will step up their game.

However, even the most passionate leader will have moments of doubt, impostor syndrome or lack of motivation. These are perfectly normal and part of the leadership journey. Whenever you feel your energy dip or are considering going back to how things used to be, revisit Chapter 1. Remind yourself of your vision, your 'why' and the type of leader you want to become. By reigniting your own passion, you will naturally inspire your team to stay engaged and aligned. Leadership is about consistency, not perfection. You don't need all the answers, but you do need to show up for your team and keep steering the ship. If you're committed to staying adaptable, celebrating progress and keeping alignment at the forefront, your team will follow suit.

Habits to keep the culture alive

Culture isn't built in a day — it's the result of the habits and practices you and your team engage in daily. These habits are the glue that keeps the momentum alive. By now, you have seen the importance of positional contracts and measurable goals and of revisiting and refreshing them regularly. You understand the power of praise and recognition. You have made your company's purpose and values visible to ensure they remain front of mind — big-picture essentials that lay the foundations of your culture.

But sometimes it's the little things that can make the biggest difference. The daily interactions with your team, regular team-building and recognition events, accessible opportunities for continuous learning and development, quarterly staff appraisals, and all-team meetings are just as vital. These consistent practices remind everyone — including you — of the progress you've already made and the results you're going for. Together, they form the core components of a winning team culture. For a detailed overview of the key habits to create an exceptional workplace for your team, visit www.takecharge-thebook.com.

Momentum is not about running at full speed all the time. It's about creating a rhythm — a cadence of reflection, course adjustments and action that keeps your business moving forward. Let momentum become part of your business's identity. Celebrate your progress, embrace the journey and watch as your team thrives in a culture that prioritises progress, alignment and success.

BOSS facts – Part 4

#13: Your team's success is your success

Michael E. Gerber's *The E-Myth Revisited* popularises a concept called the cycle of business. It's a simple but powerful idea: the business owner looks after the team, the team looks after the customers and the customers ensure the business is profitable — and a profitable business keeps the owner happy.

```
        Business
         Owner
    ↙             ↘
Business  ←——  Team
         ↖    ↙
         Customer
```

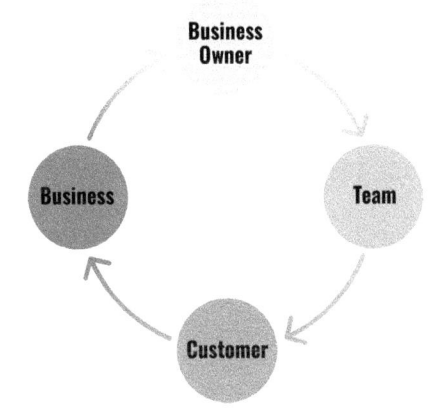

As the boss, your primary responsibility is *not* to carry every burden yourself — it's to create an environment for your team to shine. By providing the right training, support and development, your team gets equipped to deliver exceptional service and experiences for your customers. Happy customers in return become loyal, raving fans and drive the profitability and growth that keep your business afloat. When you embrace this cycle, you realise your team is your greatest asset and their success is the foundation of your business success (and by extension yours). A thriving team not only ensures a more productive and profitable business but also reflects positively on your abilities as a leader, which attracts even more great talent in the future.

However, it's important to know that no matter how motivated your team is, their emotional and financial investment will never match your own. This isn't a failure on their part; it's the reality of differing stakes. For your team, this is a job, while it's a more personal mission for you. Yet with strong leadership, a clear purpose and open communication, you can bridge this gap and create a powerful team that can't wait to contribute. Remember, your team looks to you to set the standard. That means your enthusiasm and dedication set the tone for the entire organisation. If your team perceives you as less motivated than they are, it can lead to decreased morale, loss of respect and reduced productivity. The better you lead, the better your team performs — and its success becomes a direct reflection of your leadership.

#14: Empower your team by letting go of control

As a business owner, it is oh so easy to fall into the trap of trying to do everything yourself — after all, you care deeply about your business and naturally want everything done right. But — if you are honest with yourself — you know this need for control leads to exhaustion on your part and bottlenecks in the business. Wanting to do everything yourself limits the growth of both your team and the business.

Empowering your team means trusting them to take ownership of their roles. Instead of micromanaging, focus on giving them the tools, training and autonomy they need to perform at their best. Let go of the idea that you have to oversee every decision and step in to 'fix' things or that nobody can do it the way you do. Delegation is not a sign of weakness, but it is a strategic move that frees up your time to focus on the things that matter to you.

'How can I let go of control?' I hear you ask? Easy. Start by identifying the tasks that don't require your direct involvement and delegate those to whoever holds the role that was assigned the task in Chapter 4. Communicate your expectations clearly, but avoid prescribing every step of the process (remember, people appreciate autonomy). Instead, focus on the outcome and give your team the freedom to decide how best to achieve it. Build trust through open communication and regular check-ins — not to micromanage but to support and guide (and to help you see nothing terrible is going to happen if you outsource tasks).

One key to letting go of control is recognising mistakes will happen — and that is okay. View them as learning opportunities rather than failures. Ask yourself first if your instructions were clear enough. Then offer constructive feedback and encourage your team to come up with solutions that reinforce their ability to handle challenges independently.

Over time, this practice strengthens their confidence (and yours in them) and builds a culture of ownership and accountability. If you trust your team to make decisions and support them when things don't go as planned, you create an environment where innovation and problem-solving can develop.

Ultimately, empowering your team is about stepping back to let them shine. The more you trust them, the more they will rise to the occasion — and the more time and energy you will have to focus on the aspects of your business that truly matter to you. By letting go of control, you are not losing power — you are multiplying it across the team.

#15: It's not about doing more, it's about doing what matters

When attempting to create a great office culture, it's easy to get caught up in the idea of simply doing *more*. More team-building activities, more motivational posters, more meetings about engagement strategies — because surely *more* must mean better, right? Wrong! The truth is, doing more for the sake of it won't necessarily achieve anything. Instead, focus on what really matters for *your* team. Your efforts need to be intentional and aligned with the needs of your business and the people in it. Trendy team-building activities, like trust falls, escape rooms or pizza Fridays, might be fun for some, but if they don't address the real challenges your team faces, they will only lead to eye rolls, frustration and disengagement. Instead, ask yourself: what does my team really need right now to grow, connect and shine?

For one team, this might mean hosting workshops on better communication. For another, it could be investing in tools to reduce repetitive tasks so they can focus on creative work. Perhaps your team needs a leader who makes time to check in with them individually or who recognises their efforts with genuine appreciation. Whatever the focus, it's about ensuring everything you do has a purpose that resonates with your team and contributes to your shared goals.

The same principle, by the way, applies to your personal leadership style. It's not about packing your calendar with endless meetings or working longer hours to prove your dedication. True leadership comes from doing what matters: setting clear priorities, delegating effectively and being present for the moments that make the biggest impact — whether coaching an employee, celebrating a win or realigning the team during challenging times. By focusing on what matters, you create space for the things that make a real difference: authentic connection, meaningful work and sustainable growth. So next time you're tempted to just 'do more', take a step back and ask yourself: *does this matter?* If it doesn't, let it go and focus your energy where it truly counts.

#16: The goal isn't perfection, it's progress

Here's a piece of reality for you: perfection is an impossible goal, and chasing it can actually be counterproductive. In fact, perfectionist thoughts are intertwined with anxiety and depression,[31] linked to eating disorders,[32] can lead to procrastination and burnout, and can strain your relationships.

So where does the magic happen? When you focus on progress over perfection, that's where. James Clear, in his book *Atomic Habits*, demonstrates the power of small, consistent actions. He points out that improving by just 1% every day leads to a nearly 37% improvement over the course of a year, highlighting a very simple truth: small steps forward can lead to massive gains over time.

For you as a boss, this might mean regular team check-ins to celebrate small wins rather than waiting for big, perfect outcomes. It might mean pushing forward when things aren't flawless. Instead of holding back until everything feels 'just right', get used to the idea of improving as you go. The goal here is not to produce inferior work — far from it. Instead, aim for 90% perfect and recognise that your first attempt is just a starting point — just as the saying goes, jump off the cliff and build your wings on the way down. When you encourage steady progress rather than demand perfection, you create an environment where your team feels safe to learn, grow and take initiative. Mistakes become learning opportunities, and employees are more likely to innovate and contribute. After all, progress isn't just motivating in the workplace — it's something we all love to experience in other areas of life. Think about the sense of accomplishment and motivation that comes from steadily improving at something like learning a language, going through a fitness regime or perfecting a pavlova. When people feel a sense of progress, they stay engaged, take ownership and keep pushing forward.

You know what makes progress even more meaningful? Acknowledging it. Research from Harvard Business School shows that celebrating progress is one of the most effective ways to improve morale and engagement.[33] Take time to recognise even the smallest victories and praise team members who are making meaningful steps forward. And remember, what you track improves and what you reward gets done again.

5. A Final Word: You Are Exactly What Your Business Needs

Congratulations! By working through the BOSS method, you have taken a major step towards building the business — and the team — you've always envisioned. But here's the thing: this is not a one-time exercise. This framework is a cycle, not a checklist. Your business will grow; your team will evolve and so will your challenges. And that's where the beauty of this framework lies: it is designed to grow with you.

Whenever you hit a roadblock, feel overwhelmed or find yourself losing sight of your goals, think of this book as your guide. Need a confidence boost or clarity in your leadership? Dive back into Chapter 1 and remind yourself what it takes to *be the boss your business needs*. Feeling stuck or unsure of your direction? Chapter 2 will help you refocus and *organise the ideal*. If team dynamics seem off or the engagement is dropping, revisit Chapter 3 to *survey your current reality*. And when you're ready to take action, Chapter 4 will be waiting to guide you as you *strategise and make it happen*.

This framework is here for you whenever you need it. Think of it as a toolbox you can open up, a roadmap you can follow or even a coach cheering you on from the sidelines. Building a great business is not about perfection, it's about progress, and progress is something you have already started. So keep going. Revisit the exercises, reread the BOSS facts and adapt the strategies as your business and team grow.

This is your journey, and the destination is what you make it. You are the boss now — take charge every day and keep making it happen.

As we reach the end of this journey, let's look at how far we've travelled together. From discovering whether you're a leader, a manager or a mix of both to reigniting your motivation and confidence, you've learned that being a great boss doesn't mean doing it all — it means doing what matters most. You've built your ideal version of the boss you want to be — one who is authentic, focused and resilient. We've organised your vision into something tangible and created clear roles, boundaries and structure to provide clarity and deliver results. We took a close look at your current reality and identified your team's strengths, motivators and areas for growth. Finally, we developed the strategies to bring it all to life — building a strong team culture that brings everyone onto the same page, making them motivated and unstoppable.

This book has been a roadmap to becoming the boss your business needs and, more importantly, the kind of boss your team deserves. And through it all, we have arrived at one undeniable truth: you have what it takes to build something extraordinary. As a business owner, you hold immense power — not just over the bottom line but over people's lives. You have the power to create a workplace where your team feels valued, inspired and motivated to give their best every day — a place where team members can grow into the best versions of themselves — and it's all thanks to the culture that you have created.

That is no small thing. In fact, it's one of the most impactful contributions you can make to the world. Happy teams create better businesses. Better businesses change the world for the better. So when you doubt yourself — and trust me, we all do — remember this: you're already doing the work of changing lives. Now it's about levelling up, shifting your focus from your customers to your team and creating something even bigger than yourself.

And here's the best part: you don't have to do it alone. One of the hardest things about being a business owner is the isolation that can come with it. Building something remarkable is so much easier (and more fun!) when you're surrounded by like-minded people who share your drive and vision. That's why I've created the BOSS Circle — a growing network of incredible business owners who are dedicated to growth, learning and doing things differently. It's a space where you can connect with other ambitious leaders, share ideas, ask questions and gain insights from those who have already walked the path you're on. Whether you're celebrating wins, troubleshooting challenges or looking for fresh inspiration, our community is here to support you every step of the way. Join us and become part of something bigger. Find all the details on www.takecharge-thebook.com.

Let's work together!

At The Business Fabrik, we are on a mission to change the way businesses operate by creating workplaces that people are excited to show up to every day and where business owners feel confident, supported and empowered. We don't believe in quick fixes or generic advice. Instead, we work with business owners who are serious about creating long-lasting success through meaningful change. And here's the thing — by reading this book, you have already joined the movement. You are officially a Fabrikator, and your success is now part of our mission. I am here to support you every step of the way. While I may be warm and fluffy at heart, I am fiercely committed to seeing you and your business succeed.

We only take on a select number of clients, because we believe in giving our full attention to those who are ready to roll up their sleeves and do the work. If you're looking for a partner who understands the highs and lows of leadership, knows how to build unstoppable teams and is passionate about creating change, we would love to hear from you. Working with us isn't just an investment in your business, it's an investment in your team and your future. Take the first step by visiting our website to learn more about how we can help you.

Your next steps

Here's how you can keep the momentum going and share the love:

- **Keep building a FAB business with us**: Head to www.takecharge-thebook.com to explore resources, connect with like-minded business owners and discover how we can support you in tackling your biggest leadership challenges. Whether it's through expert guidance, hands-on workshops or exclusive programmes, we're here to help you and your team thrive.
- **Leave a review of this book**: Your feedback doesn't just help others find it, it helps grow this movement.
- **Share this book with someone who needs it**: Know another boss who could use a confidence boost and a fresh perspective on leadership? Pass it along and help create better workplaces today.

Every small step you take today creates ripples of positive change. Let's take charge and make it happen.

A call to action

Now is the time to take charge and make your mark. You have the tools, the mindset and the framework to create a workplace that is not just functional but phenomenal — a place where people can't wait to show up, where they feel valued and where their work matters. Remember, your role as a leader is to create an environment where momentum isn't dependent on you micromanaging every detail. Maintaining momentum and leading your people is about consistency, celebration and continuous improvement. With these strategies in place, your team will not only meet its goals but, more importantly, enjoy the journey. Together, we can redefine what it means to be a boss. Together, we can transform businesses, build happier teams and ultimately create a better world.

The journey doesn't end here — this is just the beginning. Let's keep moving forward, one bold, fearless step at a time.

Keep it FAB, and let's change the world.

With all my support and belief in you,
Claudia

Claudia D **THOMPSON**

Acknowledgements

Writing a book has been one of the most challenging tasks I have ever undertaken: from feeling overwhelmed to losing confidence; from questioning the whole endeavour to trying (and often failing) to wrangle my ideas into a structure that made sense. There were countless moments when I was ready to give up. This book wouldn't exist — certainly not in the form it does now — without the support, encouragement and wisdom of so many people. In no particular order, I'd like to express my heartfelt thanks to the following:

To my beta readers: Andrew, Carly, Rachel and Trevor
You were the first people to read my words apart from me, and your thoughtful feedback helped shape this book into something I am truly proud of. Your insights, suggestions and encouragement gave the manuscript more depth and balance. Thank you for your time and for challenging me in the best possible way.

To Karen, my book mentor
Your guidance helped me bring order to the chaos in my mind. Thank you for helping me create structure from my jumble of ideas and for always being there to answer my questions or lend encouragement when I felt stuck.

To Sam, Catherine and the team at SWATT Books
Thank you for your tireless work editing, proofreading, typesetting and making this book look and feel exactly as it should. You have made what felt like an overwhelming process so much easier, and I am so grateful to have had you as partners on this journey.

To Claire
Thank you for taking the time to write the foreword to this book and for your amazing words. You've not only added depth and credibility to these pages but also reminded me of something truly important — that there is no competition in business, only opportunities to lift each other up. We all achieve more when we support and look out for one another and you embody that so effortlessly. Thank you for your encouragement. Keep being amazing!

To my husband, Phil
Thank you for not only supporting my dream of writing this book but for being my rock through every step of this journey. Thank you for making me talk about this book and for pushing me to own my success. I couldn't have done it without you. Most of all, thank you for being the creator of our online assessment tool, which brought one of my ideas to life in the most practical and impactful way. I couldn't have done this without you.

To Jen
My business buddy, accountability partner, the most organised person I know — and, most importantly, an incredible friend. Thank you for being my cheerleader when I needed encouragement, my sounding board when I needed clarity and my friend through it all. I am so lucky to have you in my corner.

To Diane

You have been the best teacher, colleague and team member anyone could ask for. Your kindness, calm demeanour (at least on the outside) and ability to juggle everything so it somehow all works out in the end inspire me every day.

To Ina

My sister from another mister, my voice of reason and the pillar I can always count on. Thank you for pulling me out of the rabbit holes my emotions often dig me into and for always offering a fresh, grounded perspective. Your stories and complaints about your boss were a constant reminder that bad bosses come in all shapes and sizes — and that there's so much work to be done to make workplaces better. Your support, humour and honesty have been my anchor throughout this journey, and I am endlessly grateful to have you by my side.

To Eddie

Thank you for being the first person I talked to about my business idea, for believing in its mission from the very beginning and for helping me think and dream bigger. If you are reading this, it is officially time for me to open that wine you gave me last year, which has always felt way too special to drink. I hope I have done you proud.

To Claudi, Tine and Stefan

You were the first friends I told about this book when it was close to completion and I was so incredibly nervous to share it with you. I worried about what you would think, but your reactions couldn't have been more encouraging or heartwarming. Thank you for your kindness, for your interest and for making me feel like this book was worth sharing.

To Simon

Thank you for conspiring with my husband behind my back to give me the push I needed to change my life. Our dinner where you grilled my business idea was equal parts intimidating and incredibly useful. Your questions challenged me to think deeper, refine my vision and ultimately take the leap. I am grateful for your honesty, support and belief in my idea.

To everyone else who unknowingly inspired me

There are countless people who have influenced this book in ways big and small. Whether it was a conversation, an offhand comment or simply your belief in me, you have left your mark on these pages.

Finally, **to the readers of this book**: thank you for taking a chance on these words and this message. I hope this book resonates with you and inspires you to create something better in your workplace and beyond.

Further Reading

Jim Collins, 2001, *Good to Great*

Stephen R. Covey, 2020, *The 7 Habits of Highly Effective People*

John Doerr, 2018, *Measure What Matters*

Carol Dweck, 2007, *Mindset: The New Psychology of Success*

T. Harv Eker, 2000, *Secrets of the Millionaire Mind*

Thomas Erikson, 2019, *Surrounded by Idiots*

Michael E. Gerber, 2001, *The E-Myth Revisited*

Marshall Goldsmith, 2007, *What Got You Here Won't Get You There*

Gay Hendricks, 2010, *The Big Leap*

David J. Schwartz, 2016, *The Magic of Thinking Big*

Claudia D **THOMPSON**

Take **CHARGE!**

Endnotes

1. Gallup, 2025, Global Indicator. Employee Retention and Attraction. www.gallup.com/467702/indicator-employee-retention-attraction.aspx

2. Gallup, 2025, Global Indicator: Employee Retention and Attraction. www.gallup.com/467702/indicator-employee-retention-attraction.aspx

3. The Undercover Recruiter, n.d., How Interviewers Know When to Hire You in 90 Seconds. https://theundercoverrecruiter.com/infographic-how-interviewers-know-when-hire-you-90-seconds

4. Center for Creative Leadership, 2024, Are Leaders Born or Made? Why Expectations Impact Leadership Development. www.ccl.org/articles/leading-effectively-articles/are-leaders-born-or-made-perspectives-from-the-executive-suite

5. Richard D. Arvey, Maria Rotundo, Wendy Johnson, et al., 2006, The Determinants of Leadership Role Occupancy: Genetic and Personality Factors. *Leadership Quarterly*, 17(1), 1—20. https://doi.org/10.1016/j.leaqua.2005.10.009

6   Christopher N. Cascio, Matthew Brook O'Donnell, Francis J. Tinney, et al., 2016, Self-Affirmation Activates Brain Systems Associated with Self-Related Processing and Reward and Is Reinforced by Future Orientation. *PubMed*, 11(4), 621—629. https://doi.org/10.1093/scan/nsv136

7   Nikola Baldikov, 2023, 19 Workplace Communication Statistics in 2024. Brosix, www.brosix.com/blog/workplace-communication-statistics

8   Duncan Lambden, 2024, The Importance of Effective Workplace Communication: Key Statistics. Expert Market, www.expertmarket.com/phone-systems/workplace-communication-statistics

9   Duncan Lambden, 2024, The Importance of Effective Workplace Communication: Key Statistics. Expert Market, www.expertmarket.com/phone-systems/workplace-communication-statistics

10 Nikola Baldikov, 2023, 19 Workplace Communication Statistics in 2024. Brosix, www.brosix.com/blog/workplace-communication-statistics

11 David DeSteno, 2016, Why Do Employees Trust Strangers More Than Their Own Bosses? Harvard Business Review.

12 Edelman Trust Institute, 2024, Edelman Trust Barometer: Global Report. www.edelman.com/sites/g/files/aatuss191/files/2024-02/2024%20Edelman%20Trust%20Barometer%20Global%20Report_FINAL.pdf

13 Lieke Pijnacker, 2019, HR Analytics: Role Clarity Impacts Performance. Effectory, www.effectory.com/knowledge/hr-analytics-role-clarity-impacts-performance

14 Jim Harter, 2024, In New Workplace, US Employee Engagement Stagnates. Gallup, www.gallup.com/workplace/608675/new-workplace-employee-engagement-stagnates.aspx

15 Mary Baker, 2022, 3 Ways to Set Effective Performance Goals. Gartner, www.gartner.com/smarterwithgartner/3-ways-to-set-effective-performance-goals

16 Ben Wigert and Jim Harter, 2017, Re-Engineering Performance Management. Gallup, www.gallup.com/workplace/238064/re-engineering-performance-management.aspx

17 Susan Weinschenk, 2012, The True Cost of Multi-Tasking. Psychology Today, www.psychologytoday.com/us/blog/brain-wise/201209/the-true-cost-of-multi-tasking

18 News.com.au, 2024, Recruiter Reveals the Real Reason 'Unrealistic' Gen Z Keeps Getting Fired. New York Post, https://nypost.com/2024/09/30/lifestyle/recruiter-reveals-the-real-reason-unrealistic-gen-z-keeps-getting-fired

19 Ariel Zilber, 2024, Here's Why Companies Are Rapidly Firing Gen Z Employees. New York Post, https://nypost.com/2024/09/24/business/heres-why-companies-are-rapidly-firing-gen-z-employees

20 Hermundur Sigmundsson, Monika Haga, Magdalena Elnes, et al., 2022, Motivational Factors Are Varying across Age Groups and Gender. *International Journal of Environmental Research and Public Health*, 19(9), 5207. https://doi.org/10.3390/ijerph19095207

21 Deloitte, 2023, What Motivates Workers? And, How Can You Tap into It? https://action.deloitte.com/insight/3290/what-motivates-workers-and-how-can-you-tap-into-it

22 McKinsey and Company, 2024, Women in the Workplace 2024: The 10th-Anniversary Report. www.mckinsey.com/featured-insights/diversity-and-inclusion/women-in-the-workplace

23 PWC, n.d., Millennials at Work: Reshaping the Workplace in Financial Services. www.pwc.com/gx/en/financial-services/publications/assets/pwc-millenials-at-work.pdf

24 Ford Motor Company, 2024, Working for Balance. https://corporate.ford.com/microsites/ford-trends-2024/working-for-balance.html

25 Yoon Jik Cho and James L. Perry, 2012, Intrinsic Motivation and Employee Attitudes: Role of Managerial Trustworthiness, Goal Directedness, and Extrinsic Reward Expectancy. *Review of Public Personnel Administration*, 32(4), 382–406. https://doi.org/10.1177/0734371X11421495

26 AllVoices, 2021, State of Employee Feedback 2021. www.allvoices.co/blog/state-of-employee-feedback-2021

27 AllVoices, 2021, State of Employee Feedback 2021. www.allvoices.co/blog/state-of-employee-feedback-2021

28 Richard Metcalfe, 2019, How Engaged Employees Are the Path to Success. Salesforce, www.salesforce.com/content/blogs/gb/en/2019/08/how-engaged-employees-are-the-path-to-success.html

29 Zenger Folkman, 2024, The Power of Listening Leadership: A Leader's Secret Weapon for Building Trust. https://zengerfolkman.com/articles/the-power-of-listening-leadership-a-leaders-secret-weapon-for-building-trust

30 Harvard Business Review, 2013, When CEOs Talk Strategy, Is Anyone Listening? https://hbr.org/2013/06/when-ceos-talk-strategy-is-anyone-listening

31 Jessica Lunn, Danyelle Green, Thomas Callaghan et al., 2023, Associations between Perfectionism and Symptoms of Anxiety, Obsessive-Compulsive Disorder and Depression in Young People: A Meta-Analysis. *Cognitive Behaviour Therapy, 52*(5), 460–481. https://doi.org/10.1080/16506073.2023.2211736

32 Katherine A. Halmi, Suzanne R. Sunday, Michael Strober et al., 2000, Perfectionism in Anorexia Nervosa: Variation by Clinical Subtype, Obsessionality, and Pathological Eating Behavior. *American Journal of Psychiatry, 157*(11), 1799–1805. https://doi.org/10.1176/appi.ajp.157.11.1799

33 Shibeal O'Flaherty, Michael T. Sanders and Ashley Whillans, 2021, Research: A Little Recognition Can Provide a Big Morale Boost. *Harvard Business Review,* https://hbr.org/2021/03/research-a-little-recognition-can-provide-a-big-morale-boost